For Reference

Not to be taken from this room

Food & Menu Dictionary

Food & Menu Dictionary

This edition revised, updated and expanded by
CRETE DAHL
*Hotel and Restaurant
Consultant*

Original edition by
THE DAHLS

Jule Wilkinson, Editor

CBI Publishing Company, Inc.
51 Sleeper Street
Boston, Massachusetts 02210

Illustrations on pages 38, 58, 62, 92, 101, 105 and 119, courtesy Culinary Institute of America

Printing(last digit): 9 8 7 6 5

Library of Congress Catalog Card No. 77-123002

ISBN 0-8436-0556-1

Printed in the United States of America

TABLE OF CONTENTS

DEDICATION

To good cooks everywhere!

" . . . What does cookery mean?. . . It means knowledge of all herbs, & fruits, & balms, & spices, & of all that is healing & sweet in groves, & savoury in meat. It means carefulness, willingness, & readiness of appliance. It means the economy of your great grandmother, & the science of modern chemistry, & French art, & Arabian hospitality . . . "

John Ruskin

ABOUT THE COMPILER

Crete Dahl, B. S., M. S., has had extensive experience in food preparation and service.

To begin with, she operated a restaurant. As the wife of the late J. O. Dahl, then editor of Hotel Management, Restaurant Management and Hotel-World-Review Magazines, she planned at least one new dish, or a new way of serving a familiar one, each day.

Famous guests entertained at Springbrook, the Dahls' lovely suburban home near Stamford, Connecticut, were renowned hotel and restaurant executives from all parts of the world. Celebrities included the maharaja, maharanee and princess of Indore.

Mrs. Dahl's own business travel log clocks 507,359 miles in 42 states. She has been a guest in hundreds of hotels and has patronized thousands of restaurants, collecting menus as she went along.

As president of the Dahl Publishing Co., she supervised the publication and distribution of many training manuals for hotel and restaurant employees.

In addition to being guest instructor at Cornell University's School of Hotel Administration, Crete Dahl has written nine books and manuals about hotel and restaurant operation and has edited several more. Among her important editorial achievements have been:

Menu Making for Professionals, originally written by J. O. Dahl. Completely revised and updated by Crete Dahl.

Waldorf-Astoria Manuals, four volumes covering 64 jobs in one of the world's foremost hotels. These were distributed throughout the world.

Chef's Guide to Quantity Cookery, by J. H. Breland, edited for Harper.

Professional Quantity Cooking, Basic Courses, Methods and Formulas, for the Culinary Institute of America, forerunner of INSTITUTION's *The Professional Chef.*

More recently, as editor of *Bar Management Magazine,* a Schwartz publication, Mrs. Dahl visited many important modern restaurants, cocktail lounges and bars. She interviewed leading food and beverage managers and researched production and sales of important beverages.

Food & Menu Dictionary is a book which refused to die. After the Dahl Publishing Company's supply was exhausted, orders continued to come in. Former owners wore out their books and pleaded for new copies.

In revising and enlarging the present edition of *Food & Menu Dictionary,* Crete Dahl was particularly cognizant of changes in commercial food service trends as well as in food production and processing. She recently made a multi-state survey to check on up-to-the-minute methods.

All of this experience is reflected in this updated volume of a perennial favorite, the *Food & Menu Dictionary.*

INTRODUCTION

More than two thousand menu terms are contained in this newly revised and enlarged edition of the *Food & Menu Dictionary*. They were selected from a study of several thousand menus as well as data from 400 or more food executives.

Terms most often used in menus and in food and beverage departments were chosen. Originally published in 1938, the first edition was largely devoted to foreign terms, chiefly French. Changes in the public's tastes dictated the addition of many American food terms to replace those foreign terms now seldom used in American commercial food service.

Even so, this cannot be a complete list of menu terms. Such a compilation would fill a book many times as large as this one. And it would be incomplete in a year because chefs tend to give "made-up names" to their new creations —by the hundreds.

Revisions were selected with a view to making this book useful to food and beverage managers, menu planners, chefs and cooks, headwaiters and head bartenders, waiters, waitresses, barmen and other food service personnel. It will be of special value to those who aspire to success in commercial food service and to those whose work involves food and menu terms, such as: food producers,

vii

advertising agencies, food writers, teachers and students.

Contents include a good cross-section of culinary terms:

110	Appetizers and salads
282	Baked items and desserts
133	Dairy products (cheese, eggs, milk, cream, etc.)
103	Fish and seafood
257	Meats and poultry
116	Soups, sauces and gravies
227	Terms describing food preparation, equipment and service.
263	Vegetables, fruit and nuts
327	Wines, spirits and cordials

Appendices present:
French terms commonly used in menus and recipes
Cooking and preparation terms
Measures and equivalents
Caloric values of typical alcoholic beverages

INSTRUCTIONS

Proprietary brands, trade names, bottled wines, etc., are identified with an asterisk (*) following the term.

Origin of foreign words is identified by using the first letter of the country following the listing, as "F" for French, "G" for German. "L" is used for Latin words.

Accents (diacritical marks) have been carefully compared with those given in authoritative foreign dictionaries.

Accentuation: The principal stress in a word of two or more syllables is indicated by a primary (′) placed after the syllable to be accented. A secondary accent is indicated by this same mark doubled (″). In compounds, the determinative word generally has the accent.

Terms printed with an additional "-e" (ex. Chaud -e) are adjectives or the *PAST PARTICIPLE* of a verb. The form printed is masculine, singular. Following a feminine noun, the "e" is joined to the form given in this dictionary. (ex. Chaude). (See FRENCH SPELLING).

The GENDER and FORM of FOREIGN NOUNS are identified with abbreviations, following the term. (m. sg. means "masculine, singular"; m. pl. stands for "masculine, plural"; f. sg. indicates "feminine, singular"; and f. pl. means "feminine, plural "). (See FRENCH SPELLING).

KEY TO PRONUNCIATION—ENGLISH

ă	fat, tap
ā	date, cake
â	pare, care
ä	par, bar
ĕ	set, let
ē	sweet, beet
ê	deer, beer
ẽr	over, under
ĭ	fizz, is
ī	bite, rice
ŏ	top, hot
ō	tone, scone
ô	fork, pork
o͞o	scoop, loop
o͝o	cook, book
oi	oil, boil
ou	stout, about
ŭ	cut, nut
ū	use, confuse
ũr	bur, burn

e   a in ago
         e in agent
         i in vanity
         o in come
         u in locust

ch   check, charge
sh   dash, slash
th   thick, thin
th   farther, rather
zh   measure, pleasure

KEY TO PRONUNCIATION—FRENCH

é   a as in lay
à   as in bar
â   as in pa, ma
à l'   al, or the "l" is joined to the first vowel of the next word, as in
     l'Ancien
ç   as in française, (f ran çaise)
ñ   liquid sound in Spanish, similar to yon

FRENCH SPELLING

In making up French COMPOUND TERMS the determinative word (adjective or past participle of a verb) takes the ending according to the Gender (masculine or feminine) and the Form (singular or plural of the preceding noun.

	SINGULAR	**PLURAL**
	. . . .	. . . . .s
	farci	farcis
MASCULINE	frit	frits
	braisé	braisés
	chaud	chauds
	. . . . .e	. . . . .es
	farcie	farcies
FEMININE	frite	frites
	braisé	braisées
	chaude	chaudes

Examples:

	Consommé froid	Haricots verts
m.	Chou farci	Choux farcis
	Eau froide	Pommes frites
f.	Oie farcie	Tomates farcies

FRENCH ACCENTS (é, è, ô, ç,) may be omitted on Capital letters.

xiii

Abalone (ab́ e̱ lŏ nĭ)—Large edible sea mollusk. Popular in California.

Abatis (ab́ e̱ tĭs)—Giblets.

Abricots, F. n. (ābrĭ′kō)—Apricots.

Abricotine, F. n. (ābrĭ′kō tēn)—French liqueur.

Absinthe, absinth (ăb sĭnth′)—Highly toxic liqueur running between 70-80% alcohol, blended with aromatic bitter wormwood (artemesia absinthium), Angelica Root, Anise, Hyssop, and Fennel. Said to cause hallucinations, hence outlawed in many countries. Pernod (per nō) and Herbsaint (erb săñ) are two trade-marked acceptable substitutes for combining with liquor in exotic cocktails.

Accent* (ăk sĕnt′)—Trade name for monosodium glutamate, a seasoning which brings out flavor inherent in foods without adding any flavor of its own.

Acid—Citric acid contained in oranges, lemons, limes, grapefruit; malic acid found in apples. Body processes transform these mild acids into alkalis.

Acid-forming foods which are not transformed into alkalis by the body: meats, fish, eggs, wheat products, etc.

Acidophilus*, (ăs′i dŏf e̱ le̱s)—Trade name for processed buttermilk.

Admiral Sauce—Butter sauce with anchovies, capers and lemon juice.

Agar, also called agar-agar (ā′gär)—Sea moss, a gelatin-like product which has jellying power.

Aging (ā jĭng′)—A term applied to meat held at temperatures of 34° to 36° F. to improve its tenderness. Beef is in good condition after a week or ten days; lamb or mutton in from one to three weeks; pork in two or three days.

Agneau, F. n. m. (ăn′yo)—Lamb.

Aigrefin, F. n. m. (a′gre̱ fan″)—Haddock.

Aiguilettes, F. n. f. pl. (ä gwē yet′)—Slices of meat, usually poultry.

Ail, F. n. m. sg. (eye), aulx, pl. (ails)—Garlic

Aile, F. n. f. sg. (el)—Wing, as of poultry.

Akvavit* (äkwa′vēt)—White Swedish spirits.

à la, F. (à la)—According to a style, such as à la Français, -e, meaning "according to the French way."

à l' F. (all)—Same as above. Used before words beginning with a vowel, as à l'Ancienne.

Alaska Peas—Early June peas, not necessarily from that state.

Albert Sauce—Butter sauce, white stock, horseradish, vinegar, egg yolks, seasonings.

à l'Ancienne, F. f. (à län si ĕn′)—Old-fashioned way.

à la Bordelaise

à la Bordelaise, F. (à la borde'lāz)—with Bordeaux wine.

à la Bourgeois, -ie, F. m. (à la bur'zwä) (bur'zwä si")—Plain, family style.

à la Broche, F. (à la brōsh')—Cooked on a skewer.

à la Carte, F. (à la cart')—Foods prepared to order; each dish priced separately.

à la Francais, F. (frän sā'), -caise (frän sāz')—In the French manner.

à la King—Foods served in white cream sauce containing mushrooms, green peppers and pimientos.

à la mode, F. (ä lä mōd)—Usually refers to ice cream on top of pie, but may mean other dishes served in a special way, as beef à la mode which calls for a scoop of mashed potatoes.

à la Newburg—With sauce of butter, cream, egg yolks, and sometimes sherry.

à la Normande, F. (ä lä nōr män')—Dishes with apples and fish.

à la Provencale, F. (prō vŏn säl')—Provincial. Usually dishes with garlic and olive oil.

à la Russe, R. (ä lä rōōs)—The Russian way.

Albumin—Complex proteins found in egg white, milk, muscle of lean meats, blood, fish and many vegetable tissues. Coagulated by heat. Avoid overcooking.

Alcohol—Grain alcohol is the intoxicating ingredient, distilled from grain, contained in whiskey, gin, etc. Alcohol in rum is distilled from sugar cane. Caloric value, 110 calories per ounce.

Alcoholic Beverages—Ale, beer, spirits (such as gin, whiskey, vodka, rum, liqueurs), and wines usually served in licensed establishments along with foods.

Ale—Aromatic brew made of malted cereal grain. Usually heavier and bitterer than beer.

Allemande Sauce, F. (äll män')—White sauce consisting of reduced Velouté Sauce combined with egg yolks and essence of mushrooms.

Alligator Pear—Tropical fruit. See Avocado.

Decorating foods for festive occasions is a desirable skill; a reputation for beautiful wedding cakes can attract profitable party business.

All-Purpose Flour—Blend of hard spring wheat and soft winter wheat flours.

Allumette Potatoes, F. (ăl ew mĕt')—Cut thin like match-sticks. Similar to Shoe-string Potatoes.

Allium ascalonicum, L. (ăl ē ŭm ăskä lō'nĭ cŭm)—Shallots.

Allium cepi (se pi)—Onions. Used extensively as seasoning in salads, stews, fried or roasted foods.

Allium porrum, L. (pōr' rōōm)—Leeks, usually served boiled, as a vegetable; or as a base for cream soups.

Allium scheneprasum (shĕnẹ prä'sōōm)—Chives, rush onions. Slender green onions with hollow stems. Used to season and garnish salads and other foods. Milder than ordinary onions.

Allium sativum, L. (sät ē vōōm)—Garlic, used extensively to season meats, fish, salads, dressings and sauces. Strong flavor, hence should be used sparingly. Garlic-flavored salt is a convenient and acceptable substitute for the fresh.

Allspice—Ground berry of a tree from Jamaica; used to season puddings, pies and pickles.

Almond Paste—Mixture of 56% ground blanched almonds, 34% sugar, 10% water, and flavoring.

Alose, F. n. (äl ōz')—Shad, a salt water fish.

Aloxe-Corton*, F. (ä lōx'kōr tŏn″)—Good red Burgundy wine from the villages of those two names.

Aloyau, F. m. (ălwä'yō)—Boned sirloin of beef.

Alsaçienne, à l', F. f. (äl säs yĕn')—Meat garnished with potatoes, pickled herring, thin apple slices.

Altar Wine—Good clean wine from Germany, Spain or the United States. Some churches prefer unfermented grape juice.

Amandes, F. f. pl. (ä'mänd)—Almonds.

Ambrosia—Cold dessert of bananas, shredded coconut, and oranges.

American Beauty Salad—Hard-cooked eggs, tomatoes, cream cheese. asparagus tips, lettuce.

American-fried Potatoes—Boiled potatoes, chopped fine and fried until browned on both sides.

Amer Picon*, F. (ä mĕr pē kŏn')—Trade name for a brand of aromatized wine.

Amines (ämīnō acids)—Compositions found in foods; essential for human nutrition.

Amontillado, S. (ä mŏn tē yä dō')—Very dry golden sherry.

Amoroso, S. (ä mō rō sō')—Medium sweet sherry from Spain.

Ananas, F. m. n. (ä nä näs')—Pineapple.

Ancois, F. n. m. (an swa')—Combination of white and brown sauce, Hollandaise style, with anchovy butter.

Ancienne, à l', F. (ä län si ĕn')—Old-fashioned way. Sauce: Hollandaise with cucumbers, mushrooms and truffles. Garnish: poached fish with capers, truffles, and sliced gherkins. Consommé: poultry base, croutons, Parmesan cheese.

Andalouse, à l', F. (ä län dä lōōz')—Andalusian style. Consomme and potage: tomatoes and rice. Garnish: tomatoes, boiled rice, eggplant and red peppers. Sauce: mayonnaise with tomatoes and green peppers. Salad: Spanish onions, cucumbers, tomatoes, hard-cooked eggs, oil and vinegar.

Anemia, also spelled aenemia (ă nē'miä)—Deficiency condition associated with malnutrition caused by insufficient food or incorrect combinations of foods. Symptoms: loss of weight, weakness, fatigue, etc.

Angel Food Cake—Light fluffy cake made with only the whites of eggs (no yolks). May be frosted or merely dusted with confectioner's sugar.

Angels on Horseback—Oysters wrapped in thin strips of bacon, held together with toothpicks; dipped in mixture of beaten eggs and seasonings; sauteed, then baked. Served with maitre d'hotel sauce.

Angel's Tip Cocktail (also called Angel's Tit)—Maraschino, Creme de Cacao, sweet cream, all whipped or blended into a frothy consistency.

Anglaise, à l', F. (ä lăn glāz')—English style.

Angostura Bitters* (ăn gŏs tōōrä')—Trade name for bitters used in mixed drinks, especially cocktails. Also adds piquant flavor to various foods.

Anguille, F. (än gwēēl')—Eel. See eel.

Anise (ăn iss')—Seeds for flavoring salads or savories. Essential oil is valuable for seasoning confections. Resembles licorice in taste.

Anisette*, F. (ăn e sĕt')—A brand of anise-seed cordial.

Antipasto, I. (änti päs'to)—Italian name for hors d'oeuvres. Savories served as a first course. Assortment of appetizers such as salted or pickled fish, olives, anchovies, peppers, etc., garnished with mushrooms and pimientos.

A-1 Sauce*—Trade name for bottled condiment, popularly added to meats, fish, fowl, soups and stews, either in cooking or at table.

Aperitif, F. sg. (ä pĕri tēf')—Any dry fortified wine, such as vermouth, Dubonnet, Campari, or dry sherry, which is served before a meal as an appetizer.

Apollinaris*—Brand of mineral water.

Appetizers—Beverages or assorted snacks served before a meal, or along with cocktails or wines. See aperitif, antipasto, and hors d'oeuvres.

4

Appetitost* (ä pĕti′tōst)—Danish cheese made from sour buttermilk.

Apple Blow Fizz—Drink made of Apple Jack or Apple Brandy mixed with lemon juice, sugar, and seltzer.

Apple Butter—Jam made from spiced, cooked and strained apple pulp.

Apricot Rickey—Tall drink of apricot brandy, lime juice and seltzer served over cracked ice.

Apple Snow—Dessert made of applesauce blended with beaten egg whites and sweetening. Also called a "whip."

Apple Strudel (shtrōō′del)—German specialty: baked dessert made by rolling a flaky dough around a filling of thinly sliced apples and chopped nuts, seasoned with sugar and cinnamon.

Arak* (är äk′)—Pale, straw-colored spirits from Dutch East Indies.

Armagnac*, F. (är män yăk′)—Brown French brandy.

Arrowroot—Thickening agent, similar to cornstarch, from a tropical plant of the same name. Used in delicate desserts such as blanc mange.

Asperges, F. f. pl. (ä spĕr′zh)—Asparagus.

Asparagus—Vegetable which grows as tender shoots with scale-like tips. Delicious when young and tender, boiled and served with Hollandaise or lemon-butter sauce. When tougher, asparagus may be boiled, sieved and used as a base for cream soup, etc. Available canned and frozen for year-round service.

Artichauts, F. m. pl. (är tĭ shō′)—Artichokes.

Artichokes—Globe artichokes belong to the thistle family. Grown extensively as "row crops" in California. Specialty served in the better restaurants. Boiled. Served with lemon-butter sauce or melted butter. Leaves are pulled off, dipped in sauce, and the tender lower portions are eaten. At bottom, in the center, is the artichoke heart, the most delicate part of all. See Jerusalem artichokes.

Artichoke Hearts—The fleshy bottom portion of a globe artichoke. May be purchased pickled or packed in oil. Excellent as an ingredient in fancy salads, in antipasto or hors d'oeuvres.

Assiette Parisienne, F. (ä′syĕt pärĭ′zyĕn)—Small relishes or appetizers served on a small plate, similar to antipasto or hors d'oeuvres.

Asti Spumonte*, I. (ästi spōō mŏn′tĭ)—Italian sparkling wine.

Aszu, H. (ä ts ōō)—Tokay wine from Hungary.

Aubergines, F. f. pl. (ō bĕr zhēn′)—Eggplant.

au Beurre Fondu, F. (ō bĕr fŏn dōō′)—With butter sauce.

au Beurre Roux, F. (ō bĕr rōō′)—With browned butter.

au Bleu, F. (ō blou′) Fish, plain boiled.

Auf-lauf, G.—German-type apple pudding.

au Four, F. (ō fōōr′)—Baked in the oven.

au Gras

au Gras, F. (ō grä′)—Meat with rich gravy.

au Gratin, F. (ō grǎ tăn′)—Baked with a topping of browned bread crumbs and/or grated cheese.

au Jus, F. (ō zhōō′)—Served with natural juices or gravy without thickening.

au Lait, F. (ō lā′)—With milk.

au Maigre, F. (ō mā′gre)—With food other than meat.

au Naturel, F. (ō nǎ tōō rěl′)—Plainly cooked or served raw.

Austrian Eggs—Hard-cooked eggs cut in half, yolks mixed with chopped cooked mushrooms, anchovies, oil and vinegar.

Austrian Salad—Cooked potatoes and diced apples. Served with hard-cooked eggs.

aux Croutons, F. (ō krōō tŏn′)—Served with bread diced and fried in butter. Garnish for soups.

Avocado, Alligator Pear, Calavo*—Large pear-shaped fruit with green or purplish skin, filled with buttery pale-green pulpy flesh growing around a large hard pit. Originally from tropical America and West Indies. Now raised extensively in California. Sometimes called Calavo, a trade name. May be sliced or diced in deluxe salads, or mashed to a paste and seasoned for cocktail-hour dips. Luxury entree when stuffed with salad of crab, shrimp, lobster or chicken; especially delightful as a luncheon specialty.

A striking color combination is created when deep pink shrimp are placed against pale green avocado flesh.

B&B—Liqueur blend of half-and-half Brandy and Benedictine.

Baba au Rhum Chantilly, F. (bäbä ō rŭm′shăn tē yē)—Small cakes with rum flavor or soaked in rum and topped with whipped cream.

Bacardi* (bä kär′dē)—Brand of rum formerly made in Cuba from sugar cane. Now made in Puerto Rico and Hawaii.

Bacardi Cocktail—Rum, lime juice and grenadine shaken over shaved ice. A spritz of lime rind adds piquancy.

Bacardi Habanero Cocktail (hä bänyĕrō′)—Rum, sweet cream and Creme de Cacao, shaken over shaved ice to a smooth blend.

Baclava—Russian or oriental pastry made of flaky dough, honey, butter and chopped nuts.

Bain marie—Steam table with cutouts to hold pans of food at desired temperatures. Also a double boiler.

Bagratin, F. (bä grä tăn′)—Fish soup with vegetables.

Baked Alaska—Brick ice cream on cake covered with meringue and browned quickly in the oven.

Baked beans—Small dried "Navy" beans soaked overnight and baked slowly with tomato sauce, molasses and salt pork or bacon. A Saturday night regular in parts of New England. See Beans Boston-style.

Baking—Cooking with indirect heat in an oven.

Baliki (bä le′kē)—Russian dish of smoked sturgeon.

Balm (bäm)—An herb resembling lemon in taste. Leaves are used for seasoning meats, fish and salads.

Bamboo Cocktail—Dry sherry and Italian vermouth.

Bamboo Shoots—Young sprouts of the bamboo plant, used in Chinese dishes.

Bananas—Tropical fruit which may be served whole raw, sliced over dry cereals or mixed in fruit salads or fruit cups. Or bananas may be split lengthwise and used as a base for ice cream desserts, or baked in liqueurs. Mashed, they may be used as an ingredient in banana cake, banana bread or muffins.

Bananes, F. f. pl. (bä nän′)—Bananas.

Banbury Tarts—A strip of pastry folded as a triangle or semi-circle and filled with a mixture of raisins, sugar, cracker crumbs, egg yolk, lemon juice and grated lemon rind. Baked in hot oven.

Bannock—Quick Scotch bread of corn meal, eggs, and milk.

Banuti (bă nōō′tē)—Dessert of bananas, nuts, sugar, lemon juice and whipped cream.

Barbeau, F. m. (bär bō′)—Bass, found in both fresh and salt waters.

Barbeque or barbecue

Barbeque or barbecue—Roasting over direct flame or under direct heat similar to broiling, but basting with well-seasoned barbecue sauce.

Barbecue Sauce—Ketchup, onion, garlic, vinegar, butter, sugar, salt, pepper, and Worcestershire Sauce, all blended into a basting liquid. It may also be served as a condiment over barbecued meats.

Barbera* (bär bĕr′ä)—Red Italian wine.

Barbue or barbillon, F. f. (bär bo͞o or bär′bē yŏn″)—Brill, a salt water fish.

Bardé, or ée, F. (bär dä′)—Larded.

Barelas Eggs—Baked eggs in highly seasoned Mexican Sauce.

Bar le Duc (bär le do͞ok′)—Famous jam of red currants. Piquant flavor.

Barley, Pearl—Polished barley grain. The sort usually used in cooking.

Barley—Grain similar to wheat. Used as a base for malt (sprouted barley) in brewing beer and ale; also combined with other grains in the manufacture of whiskey.

Barolo* (bär ō′lō)—Red Italian wine.

Barracuda (bär ä ko͞o′dä)—Large salt water fish with white flesh. Pike-like. Lives in tropical waters. Edible.

Barsac*, F. (bär săk′)—White Bordeaux wine.

Basil (băz′l)—Herb of the mint family. Leaves (green or dried) may be used for flavoring salads and savory foods.

Basting (bāst ing)—Moistening a roast with water, drippings, or seasoned sauce while it is roasting to prevent it from drying out or scorching. Improves flavor.

Batter (băt′r)—Mixture of flour and liquid to a consistency that can be stirred and poured, as for cake, griddle cakes, flapjacks. Also used as a dip for coating fruit or vegetables for frying or deep frying.

Batter Bread—Southern dish of corn meal, hominy grits and eggs.

Bavarian Cream—Standard gelatin jelly except that half of the liquid is cream, which is whipped and folded in after the mixture begins to congeal. Mixture of whipped cream and beaten egg white may be used if preferred.

Bay Leaves—Dried leaves of the sweet bay tree grown in Italy and Greece. Used to flavor meats, soups, sauces, and pickling liquids.

Beans, Boston-style—Similar to baked beans except that small pea beans are used. Dry mustard added. After soaking overnight, they are par-boiled slowly, cooking just below the boiling point to prevent the skins from bursting. Baked slowly for 7 or 8 hours.

Beans, Pinto—Speckled flat beans, said to be more tender than other types.

Bean Sprouts—Mung beans from China. Sprouts are used when tiny, tender and green in making Chinese dishes.

Béarnaise Sauce, F. (bâr nāz')—Yellow sauce made of egg yolks, fat, onion-juice, chopped tarragon and parsley, salt and pepper, and tarragon vinegar. Light, fluffy, smooth; cooked in a double boiler. May also be used as a base for other sauces.

Beaten Biscuits—Southern specialty made of flour, milk, shortening, salt and sugar. Rolled thin, beaten with rolling pin, folded over and beaten repeatedly. Then rolled thin, shaped with biscuit cutter and baked. Flaky texture.

Beaujolais*, F. (bō″zhō lā')—Red Burgundy wine.

Bechamel Sauce, F. (bā′shăm ĕl″)—Popular sauce made of diced onions and carrots sautéed in butter before adding chicken or veal stock. Seasoned with bay leaves, parsley and peppercorns. Thickened with flour-and-butter roux. After milk is added, sauce is cooked until smooth and thick, then strained. Served over croquettes, soufflés, and instead of cream sauce for chicken, etc.

Beef—Meat from cattle more than a year old. Steer meat is the most tender beef.

Beef à la mode—Round steak or brisket cooked with onions, carrots, vinegar and spices. May be served with a scoop of mashed potatoes.

Beef à la Stroganoff, French name for a Russian dish, (strō′găn öff)—Beef tenderloin sautéed and finished with sour cream sauce. Poured over boiled noodles. May be bought as a combination package, complete with wide noodles and sauces, with only meat to be added. Ground meat is suggested. A delicious quick meal.

Beef, Baby—Meat from heifers and steers which are less than a year old, hence tender.

Beef, Dried—Meat which has been soaked in salt brine, then smoked and dried. Long "keeping quality." Usually sliced very thin. May be used for sandwiches, mixed with scrambled eggs, or flaked for mixing with cream sauce to be poured over toast, boiled rice or mashed potatoes.

Beefsteak d'Aloyau, F. (däl ō yō')—See Porterhouse Steak.

Beef Zingara—Russian specialty of potted beef preserved in wine. Served with chicken livers, mushrooms, eggs and vegetables.

Beelzebub (bēel′zēe bŭb)—Canapé spread of chopped mixed vegetables served on toasted bread crescents.

Beer—Beverage made of malted cereal grain (usually barley), hops and water. Amber color. Effervescent. Lower alcoholic content than distilled liquors. See Lager Beer. Fermentation creates the carbonic bubbles.

9

Beer, Birch—Beverage made of the sweet sap of the black birch tree. Carbonated soft drink.

Beer, Bock (bŏk)—Rich dark beer of barley, wheat, roasted malt, and hops. Fermented, hence carbonated.

Beer, Dark—Same as other beer except that in this brew the malt is roasted.

Beer, Draft—Served direct from the keg. Said to be livelier than bottled or canned beer. Now draft beer is also available in bottles.

Beer, Lager (German word meaning "to lay, rest or settle." Pronounced lä′ge͞r)—Light sparkling beer with lively quality resembling carbonated beverages.

Beets, Strawberry—Small red beets, widely used as a vegetable, in salads or pickled. In 1971, Burpee introduced golden beets which are said to be non-staining.

Beignets, F. m. pl. (bā nē ā)—Fritters.

Bellevue Salad Dressing—Thousand Island Dressing blended with whipped cream.

Bel Paese* Cheese, I. (bĕl′pä ĕsä)—Italian cheese made of cow's milk. Soft texture. Good served with crackers instead of, or after, dessert.

Benedictine*, F. (bĕnĕ dĭk te͞en)—Cordial made by the Benedictine Monks. An elegant liqueur. See B&B.

Bercy Sauce, F. (bear′se͞)—Parisian favorite which gives flavor without thickening. Mixture of chopped shallots or chives combined with minced parsley, melted butter, lemon juice and white wine. Used for eggs, fish, calf's liver and many other foods.

Beri-beri—An Asiatic deficiency disease caused by lack of vitamin B in the diet. Symptoms: weakness and wasting away. Source of vitamin B: milk, eggs, liver, kidney, fruit, leafy vegetables, yeast.

Bermuda Rose Cocktail—A colorful drink of gin, peach brandy, orange juice and grenadine.

Bernkastler Doktor, G. (bairn kăst′ler dōk″tôr)—Considered to be the best Moselle wine. Comes from a choice vineyard located along the Moselle River in Germany. This wine is considered supreme!

Beurre, F. m. (bu͞r)—Butter.

Beurre Fondu, F. (bu͞r fŏn do͞o′)—Melted butter.

Beurre Noir, F. (bu͞r nwär′)—Browned butter sauce, sometimes combined with vinegar or lemon juice. Seasoned with salt and pepper and garnished with chopped parsley.

Beurre Roux, F. (bu͞r ro͞o′)—Browned butter thickened with flour and cooked until flour is done.

Biftek, F. (bĭff tĕk)—Beefsteak.

Bigarde Sauce, F. (bē gärd′)—Orange juice and grated rind, duck drippings, white wine, salt; thickened with flour and served with roast duck. (Hot or cold duck.)

Bisque Glacé, or biscuit glacé, F. (glä sä′)—Frozen dessert of whipped cream, sugar, eggs, and vanilla. Molded in fancy shapes. Party dessert.

Bisque Tortoni, also biscuit Tôrtōnĭ, F. (hēs kwēt tôr tō′nĭ)—Vanilla ice cream blended with crushed macaroons and frozen in little frilled paper cups. A mini-dessert which provides just enough sweet to follow a big meal.

Bisque, F. f. (bēēsk)—Thick cream soup, usually of shell fish. English pronunciation: "bisk."

Bisque Ice Cream—Ice cream with high butter-fat content, mixed with crushed macaroons or crumbled sponge cake and refrozen.

Bitki à la Cossak, R. (bĭt′kē à lä kō säk)—Russian dish of round croquettes served with onions, mushrooms, and sauce, en casserole.

Bitochki, R. (bĭt ōch′kē)—Russian favorite of chicken and veal croquettes with vegetables.

Bitter Chocolate—Baker's chocolate with low sugar content (5% to 20%).

Blackstrap Molasses—Dark, thick syrup produced during the process of making sugar from the sap of sugar cane. Blackstrap is unrefined. Liked by health food fans. Similar to British treacle which is said to have curative qualities.

Blanc, F. m. (blän), blanche, F. f. (blänsh)—White.

Blanched Almonds—Scalded to remove skins. Crisped by frying in butter.

Blanc Mange, F. (blän mänzh′)—Delicate pudding served with stewed fruit, or over stale cake.

Blanquette, F. (blän kĕt′)—White fricassée.

Blanquette d'Agneau, F. (blän kĕt′dän yō)—Stewed lamb with white sauce. Usually shoulder or breast.

Blazers, pl.—Winter drinks. Served flaming.

Blender—Electrical mixer for thorough blending and aerating of drinks, such as malted milk, fancy cocktails to be served frothy, etc.

Blending—Thorough mixing of two or more ingredients.

Bleu Fromage, F. (ble frōm äzh′)—Blue cheese, like Roquefort, but made from cows' milk instead of sheeps' milk.

Blinchiki, R. (blĭn′chē kē)—Russian pancakes made of flour, eggs, milk. Fried in butter and served with sour cream, jam, jelly or powdered sugar. May be stuffed with applesauce, jelly or cottage cheese.

Blintzes

Blintzes—Thin pancakes rolled around a filling of cream cheese, chopped meat or fruit.

Blitz Torte, G. (blĭtz tōr′tĕ)—German cake of almonds, eggs, etc.

Bloaters—Half-dried smoked salt herring.

Bodenheimer*, G. (bō′dĕn hĩmer″)—German Rhine wine.

Boeuf, F. m. (buff)—Beef.

Boiled Dressing—Salad dressing (served hot or cold) of blended sugar, flour, salt, pepper, eggs, vinegar, dry mustard, milk, butter and paprika, cooked to a smooth pouring consistency. Especially good for cold slaw (also called "cole-slaw").

Boiling—Process of cooking foods in water at 212°F. See simmering.

Bologna, I. (bō lō nē, or colloquially, bälōney)—Sausage of beef and pork, highly seasoned and stuffed in casings, then smoked. Originated in Bologna, Italy.

Bombay Duck—Dried East Indian fish, similar to sardines in size. Considered a delicacy. Served with curried dishes.

Bombe, F. (bŏmb)—Ice cream molded in globular form.

Bombe Glaçé, F. (bŏmb glä sä′)—Round mold or melon lined with one kind of ice cream and filled with another.

Bon Air*, F. (bŏn air′)—Bordeaux Claret from France.

Bonito, (bŏn e′tō)—Fish of the mackerel family, found in salt water.

Bonne Femme, F. f. (bōn fĕm′)—Literally means "good wife." Term used to indicate simple family-style or home-style. Consomme or potage: with potatoes, leeks, carrots, onions. Garnish: with onions, shallots and mushrooms.

Boula Boula, (bōō lä bōō lä)—An exotic combination of green turtle soup and concentrated green pea soup; served hot with unsweetened whipped cream on top, browned under the broiler.

Borage (bōr ĭj)—Herb plant whose green or dried leaves are used for seasoning.

Bordeaux, F. (bōr dō′)—French wine from the Bordeaux region.

Bordelaise, a la, F. (bōr′dĕl äz)—With Bordelaise Sauce.

Bordelaise Sauce, F. (bŏr′dĕl az)—White or brown sauce made of beef bouillon, lemon juice, butter, herb bouquet, finely-minced shallots, salt, pepper, and flavored with Bordeaux wine.

Bordure, F. f. (bōr dyur′)—Border or ring (as of rice or mashed potatoes) for garnishing hot foods; cake or gelatine used for fancy puddings and desserts.

Borscht, or borcht, R. (bôrsh)—Russian soup usually served cold. Made of chopped fresh beets, onions, lemon juice or vinegar, salt and pepper, water or soup stock. Topped with sour cream. Juice of boiled onions may be substituted for raw onions. Sometimes chopped cabbage is added. Garnish with a spoonful of sweet cream is optional.

Borovika* (bō rō vē′kä)—Polish distillate flavored with juniper extract.

Boston Brown Bread—Baked round loaf made with a combination of white and whole-wheat flour, corn meal, baking powder and baking soda, dark molasses, sugar, salt, and seedless raisins. May also be bought already baked, in cans. Good as a snack when sliced thin and spread with cream cheese. Buttered slices of Brown Bread are standard with Boston Baked Beans.

Boston Cream Pie—Two-layer cake with custard or whipped cream filling and powdered or confectioner's sugar sprinkled on top.

Botulus Bacilli, also called **Bŏtūlinŭs**—Bacteria which secrete poisonous substance in the presence of oxygen. May be found in improperly canned foods, in fresh or cooked foods which are inefficiently refrigerated or are left exposed to air at room temperature or warmer. Food deliveries should not be left standing unprotected, but should be stored properly at once.
Prevention: Examine cans and jars for air-tightness. Discard bulged or leaking cans. Boil canned foods and soups before serving, even when they are to be served chilled. Cover all foods before refrigerating to prevent contamination from other foods which may be spoiled, and cause botulism.
Commercial food purveyors must be especially careful. For example, one death caused by contaminated vichysoisse forced its producer, a century-old cannery, into bankruptcy in 1971.

Bouchée, F. f. (bōō shā′)—Small pastry shell filled with minced or creamed meat, fish, chicken or lobster.

Bouillabaise, F. (bōō′yä bāz″or bōō′yä bĕss″)—Provence dish made like a wine-flavored stew, containing an assortment of fish and seafood, such as bass, trout, salmon, cod, snappers, lobster, crabs, eel, ray, etc. Saffron or tomato may be used for coloring. A New Orleans specialty although served in fine restaurants nationally. Example: a New York restaurant serves it every Friday routinely, and on special order any day.

Bouilli, F. (bōō yē′)—Boiled.

Bouilli d'Avoine, F. (bōō yē′dä vwän′)—Porridge.

Bouillon, F. m. (bōō yŏn′)—Beef broth. Also available in dry form, granulated or pressed into cubes to which hot water is added. May be used as a low-calorie soup or added to other foods to impart flavor.

Boulangere, à la, F. (bōō län zhair′)—With diced potatoes and fried onions.

Bouquet Garni, F. (bōō ka gä ne′)—Mixture of herbs tied together and used to flavor soups and sauces. The flavor is extracted without serving the leaves.

Bouquetiere, à la

Bouquetiere, à la, F. (boo kä tē air´)—With a variety of vegetables in season.

Bourbon (bûr´bŏn)—Also called "Corn Whiskey." Name applies to any whiskey which is distilled from a mash of grain containing not less than 51% corn grain. American made. Kentucky origin, Bourbon County. Indispensable ingredient in the famous Kentucky Mint Juleps.

Bourgeois, -ie, à la, F. (boor zwähz or boor zwäsie)—Family style, such as meats served with buttered potatoes, carrots, glazed onions, and/or garnished with bits of crisply-fried bacon.

Bouteille, F. f. (boo tä´)—Bottle.

Bread-fruit—Sweet starchy fruit from a tropical tree of the same name. Round green. Bread-like when baked. Found on South Pacific islands.

Braise, -e, F. (brāz)—To brown meat, fish or vegetables in a small amount of fat. Then liquid is added and the whole cooked, covered, on top of the range or in the oven.

Braising—Cooking slowly in a small amount of liquid.

Braziere, F. (brā zeer´)—Oval stew pan with handles at each end. Covered.

Brandy—Distilled wine or fermented fruit juices. The French call it "the soul of the wine." Originally developed to extract water from wine for shipping from France to America to reduce transportation cost. Water was to be re-added on arrival. But brandy proved so popular that it became a separate class of liquor.

Brandy Blazer—After-dinner drink, served flaming. Brandy, cube sugar, lemon or orange peel.

Brandy Cobbler—Brandy, fruit, sugar, seltzer.

Brandy Cocktail—Brandy, Curacao, Angostura Bitters.

Brandy Julep—Julep with brandy instead of the traditional Bourbon. A specialty drink.

Brandy Smasher—Brandy, fresh mint, sugar.

Bratwurst, G. (brät´voorst)—German sausage.

Brauneberger* (brown ĕ bĕrger)—German Moselle wine; among the sweetest and least sharp of the region.

Braunschweiger*—Brand of smoked liverwurst.

Bread Flour—Made of hard, or spring, wheat.

Breads—Breads may be thought of merely as baked loaves of yeast-raised dough. Or, breads may be looked upon as menu items of great promotional value. Great variety is available, such as:

White breads: buttermilk, potato, sandwich, farm-style, home-style, fortified, protein, split-top, Italian, French, Vienna, twists.

Whole-grain and graham: stone-ground, cracked wheat, whole grain berry, whole wheat, whole grain raisin, pumpernickel, Bavarian, gluten, oat, oatmeal.

Rye breads: light, black, wheat-free, party, Russian, Swedish, Bohemian, Jewish, caraway.

Specialty breads: nutbread, banana loaf, peanut butter, butter-nut, upside-down white, upside-down whole-wheat, upside-down sandwich, coffee, almond, cinnamon, bread-sticks.

Hot breads: English muffins (yeast-raised dough), sour-dough muffins, corn meal, whole-wheat, graham, blueberry, nut, etc.

Rolls made of yeast-raised dough: crescent, clover, dinner, Parker House, Brown-n-Serve, hard rolls, etc.

Sweet rolls: (breakfast or lunch): honey-buns, Danish, cheese, cinnamon, custard, raisin, pecan, caramel, etc.

The less bread is baked in homes, the more keenly patrons are attracted to restaurants which make a point of serving a tempting variety.

Brick Cheese—Ripened semi-hard cheese made of whole milk. Has many small round holes.

Brie*, F. (brēē or brēē ā′)—Soft, flavorful cheese from France.

Brillante*, S. (brēē lyän′tā)—White Spanish wine.

Brine—Liquid of salt, water and vinegar used for pickling meats or vegetables.

Brioche, F. (brēē ōsh′)—Usually refers to small pear-shaped rolls of raised dough made with yeast, eggs, milk, butter, and flour. Light.

Brisket—Meat cut from breast of an animal.

Broccoli (brä kō lē′)—Italian vegetable resembling green cauliflower. Served boiled and garnished with Hollandaise Sauce or butter sauce, creamed or en casserole.

Broche, F. (brōsh)—Metal skewer or spit. See Brochette.

Brochet, F. (brō shā′)—Pike, a fresh water fish.

Brochette, F. (brō shĕt′)—Meat broiled and served on a skewer to hold in place while cooking. Sometimes meat is combined with sections of fresh tomatoes, mushrooms, onions, green peppers, etc. Brass Rail Restaurants serve Shishkabobs on a sword-like spike which the patron may take home.

Broiling—To cook by exposing food to intense direct heat, as beneath the broiler unit of a range or over charcoal as in specialty steak-houses. Pan broiling: cooking with little or no fat on top of the range.

Bronx Cocktail—Gin, vermouth, orange juice.

Brown Betty—Apple pudding made with bread crumbs, sliced apples or applesauce, melted butter, sugar or molasses, juice and grated rind of a lemon or orange, cinnamon or other spices. May be made with any fruit. Served hot, with cream, whipped cream or a preferred sauce.

Brownies (cookies)—Chocolate, nuts, butter, eggs, flour and sweetening. Baked in a flat pan and cut into squares when cool.

Brown Rice—Unpolished rice. Contains more vitamins than the white or polished kind.

Brown Sauce—Fat is allowed to brown before flour is added; the mixture, or roux, is browned before liquid is added. Has many uses. Flavor varies according to the kind of fat used (butter, cooking oil, olive oil, roast drippings, residue of fried meats, etc.)

Brown Stew—Meat is browned in a little fat before water is added.

Brule, F. (brool)—Molded pudding of cornstarch, eggs, milk and whipped cream.

Brunoise Sauce, F. (brun'wäz)—*The Professional Chef's* recipe calls for cooking beef and veal bones in an oven, adding beef fat, and an assortment of vegetables such as carrots, onions, and tomatoes, plus a mixture of seasonings (garlic, cloves, thyme, peppercorns, and chopped parsley). Vealstock may be added. From this base several other sauces may be made such as mushroom sauce, piquante, cider, onion, and pickle.

Brut, F. (broot or brŭt)—Dry, said of wines or champagne. Not sweet.

Bubble and Squeak—Corned beef and cabbage.

Buck—Sheep over two years old.

Buck, Barbadoes—Exotic 16-oz. cooler made with both light and dark rums, lime juice, and ginger beer over ice.

Buck Rabbit—Welsh rarebit with poached eggs.

Buffet (boo fä')—Display of ready-to-eat foods. Self-service from a table of assorted foods. Similar to Smorgasbord.

Buffet Russe (boo fä roos')—Russian buffet with caviar, etc.

Bungalow Salad—Romaine, chicory, cress, cucumbers, tomatoes, radishes.

Burgundy, F. (bur'gŭn dee)—Clear French wine (white or red) from the Bourgogne region of France. Also produced in California.

Burnet—Herb whose young leaves make zesty seasoning for salads.

Buttermilk—Sour liquid left after butterfat has been removed in churning butter. May also be artificially-curdled milk.

Butternut—Hard-shelled American nut with large rich kernel. Used in mixture of salted nuts.

Butterscotch Pie—Open-faced pie topped with whipped cream or non-dairy substitute. Filling is made of brown sugar, eggs, butter, cornstarch and milk or water. Prepared Butterscotch Pudding may be made with milk and poured into pre-baked crust.

Butterscotch Sauce—Made of white or brown sugar, corn syrup, butter and flavoring. Used as topping for ice cream or puddings, if cooked thin; as cake frosting, if cooked until thick enough to spread smoothly.

Byrrh* (beer)—Trade name for a French tonic wine.

In Britain it's Bubble and Squeak but in the U. S. A. it's Corned Beef and Cabbage—usually slices of corned beef accompanied by a wedge of cooked cabbage, often with a boiled potato as well.

Cabillaud, F. m. (kä bēē yō′)—Cod. See Cod.

Cabinet Pudding—Gelatin, milk, eggs, macaroons, combined with whipped cream and chilled in a mold.

Cacciatori, I. (cä chyä tōrǐ′)—Chicken casserole cooked with olive oil and vegetables. Famous Italian dish which used to be made of wild poultry. "Cacciatori" means "hunter's."

Cadillac*, F. (kăd′yăk)—White Bordeaux wine.

Cacao (käkä′o or kă kā′ō)—A bean or seed of a tropical evergreen tree from which cocoa and chocolate are made. Also a liqueur used in fancy, sweet, cream-type cocktails.

Café, F. (kă fä′)—May mean coffee, a coffeehouse, or a restaurant serving alcoholic beverages along with food; sometimes providing entertainment as well.

Café Brulé, F. (kă fä′brōō lä′)—After-dinner coffee with brandy and sugar.

Café au lait, F. (kă fä′ō lä′)—Coffee with hot milk. Traditional French breakfast drink.

Café au Kirsch—Black coffee with Kirschwasser (Cherry Brandy).

Café Frappé, F. (frä pä′)—Frozen coffee sweetened and served with whipped cream.

Café Noir, F. (nwär)—Black coffee.

Café Royale, F. (roy äll′)—After-dinner coffee with Cognac or other brandy.

Café Turque, F. (turk)—See Turkish Coffee.

Caffeine (kă fēēn′)—Alkaloid present in coffee, tea and cocoa which is a mild stimulant to the heart and central nervous system. Ingredient which makes black coffee a traditional "sober-upper."

Caille, F. (ky)—Quail, a small game bird. Delicacy.

Calories—The units used to measure the energy produced by food when oxidized by the body. Excess calories are converted into fat. Weight-conscious customers habitually count calories in foods offered on the menu before they order.

Calavo*—Trade name for avocados grown in Cálifornia.

Calf's Liver—Choice delicacy usually served broiled or pan-broiled in slices ¼ in. thick, with crisply fried bacon and/or cooked onions. Rich in iron, which is prized by anemics or convalescents.

Calvados*—French Apple Jack or Apple Brandy.

Camembert Cheese, F. (kä mäm bĕr′)—Soft, creamy cheese produced in France. Crusty outer layer is also eaten by connoisseurs.

Camembert is also produced in the United States. Usually sold in foil-wrapped wedges.

Calendula or Pot Marigold—So-called because it blooms "around the calendar," i.e. almost all year. Fresh petals garnish salads. Dried petals or florets yield yellow dye or coloring matter for butter, cheese, and other foods such as "Marigold Buns." Substitute for saffron. Dried powdered florets give pleasant aroma to soups, meats, fish and venison.

Camomile—Herb of the aster family. Dried flowers are used for a tonic tea; also an emetic.

Canadian Bacon—Trimmed, pressed, smoked loin of pork. Lean.

Canadian Meat Pie—Round steak, lamb, kidneys, vegetables, and seasoning baked in a casserole or deep dish with pastry cover.

Canapé, F. (kă nä pä′)—Toasted bread or crackers spread with savory paste and garnished for eye-appeal. Appetizers served with cocktails. See Hors d'Oeuvres.

Canard, F. (kă när′)—Duck.

Canard Sauvage, F. (sō väzh′)—Wild duck.

Candied—See Candying.

Candying—Cooking fruit in heavy syrup until transparent, then draining and drying it. Candied yams or sweet potatoes are boiled first, then glazed in thick syrup and served that way.

Canestrato*, I. (cän ĕs trätō′)—Italian cheese from Sicily. Made of goats' milk and cured for a year before serving.

Caneton, F. m. (kän tŏn′)—Duckling.

Cannibal Sandwich—Freshly-ground tenderloin of beef served uncooked with raw egg dropped carefully on top. Garnished with chopped onions, anchovies and capers.

Cantaloup, or cantaloupe (kăn tẹ lōp′)—Melon with hard, ribbed or netted rind and sweet, juicy orange-colored flesh. Served chilled in halves or sections as a breakfast-starter or an appetizer before lunch or dinner. May also be scooped in little balls for fruit cups or diced for fruit salads. Halves filled with ice cream make choice desserts. Similar to muskmelon.

Capers—Green buds of a Mediterranean bush, pickled and used to flavor or garnish salads and other foods. Brine may add flavor to sauces.

Capon—Castrated rooster, which grows larger than the average chicken (5 to 7 lbs.). More tender than other roosters.

Capri*, I. (kä′prēē)—Italian wine from the Isle of Capri.

Caprice Salad—Orange sections or dices, tomatoes, green peppers arranged on a bed of crisp lettuce. Decorated with paprika. Cream dressing.

Capsicum

Capsicum—Pod of a tropical plant of the pepper family. Gastric stimulant. Used whole, cut up, pickled or dried and powdered. Mild peppers make paprika. "Hot" ones produce cayenne.

Caramel Sauce—Thick sauce of dark sugar cooked until brown. Thin: good over ice cream, custards and puddings. Thick: as caramel frosting on cakes or cupcakes.

Caramelizing—The process of cooking sugar until it turns brown, for use as flavoring or for coloring foods.

Caraway—Brown small crescent-shaped seeds from Denmark or Holland, used for rye bread and some cheeses.

Carbohydrates—Compounds found in sugar, starches and celluloses. In vegetables: potatoes, corn, rice and beans are rich in carbohydrates. Also present in wheat and other cereal grains. Noodles, pastas and pastries also contain considerable quantities of carbohydrates. Eaten sparingly by dieters.

Cardamom, cardamon, cardamum—Asiatic herb of the ginger family. Its seed is used as a spice. Some detectives claim it conceals "liquor breath."

Cardinal Sauce—Béchamel Sauce with shrimp or lobster roe and lemon juice.

Cardoon—Plant with edible stalks; in the globe artichoke family.

Carotene—Orange or yellow compound found in carrots and certain other vegetables. Changed into vitamin A in the body. See vitamins.

Carp—Fresh-water fish living in ponds or other tranquil waters. Similar to goldfish. Edible.

Carré de Mouton, F. (kä rā de moo′tŏn)—Rack of mutton.

Carrot Sticks or Straws—Carrots cut into thin strips or sticks. Chilled and served in salads or with celery and olives as appetizers.

Carte du Jour, F. (cärt doo joor′)—Menu or bill of fare for the day.

Carrottes, F. pl. (kä rŏt′)—French for carrots.

Casaba Melon—Large oval melon with lemon-yellow rind and whitish flesh. In season from September to April.

Cashew Nut—Small kidney-shaped rich tropical nut. Roasted and salted, it is combined with other nuts or served alone with appetizers or at the end of a meal.

Cassia—Herb grown in the tropics. Pods are used for seasoning. Taste is similar to cinnamon. Mildly laxative.

Casserole, en casserole—A dish in which food may be oven-cooked and served without transferring to another dish.

Catawba Sparkling Wine*—Sweet sparkling American wine made from red Catawba grapes. Similar to Pink Champagne.

Catsup or ketchup—Seasoned condiment made with tomatoes, onions and spices. Similar to Chili Sauce, but strained. Popular over hamburgers, wieners, baked beans, meats generally, and even French-fried potatoes.

Caudle—Scotch gruel with eggs and liqueur, wine or ale added. A warm drink for invalids.

Caviar, R. (kä've är)—Russian delicacy consisting of salted roe (eggs) of sturgeon, salmon or certain other fish. Black caviar, imported from Russia, is the most expensive and also the most prized for "posh" parties. Red caviar is widely used for appetizers, canapés and hors d'oeuvres. A symbol of "living it up." Usually served ice cold as a spread for crackers, accompanied by finely chopped hard-cooked eggs and minced onions. The latter optional.

Cayenne Pepper (kī ĕn')—Very hot red pepper made by grinding dried seed or pods of capsicum. See capsicum.

Céleri, F. (sĕl rĭ')—Celery.

Celeriac—Variety of celery grown for its turnip-like root instead of for the blanched stalks. Its flavor is similar to that of celery. Tops are trimmed off. Bulbs are washed and pared, then boiled for about half an hour. Hot, celeriac may be creamed or scalloped. Cold, it may be used in salads.

Celery—A plant whose blanched crisped stalks are eaten as a vegetable. Fresh raw celery stalks are standard appetizers. Celery may also be cut up, boiled and served with butter or cream sauce. Imparts flavor when added to casserole dishes. Leaves are customarily boiled with onions and other vegetables to flavor soups.

Celery Curls—Thin strips of celery chilled in ice water until they curl. Served as appetizers along with carrot sticks, olives, cauliflower florets, etc.

Celery Salt—Ground celery seeds combined with table salt and used to flavor soups and stews.

Celestine, F. (sä lĕs tēen') Consomme with slices of unsweetened pancakes.

Cepes, F. pl. (sĕp)—Species of mushrooms.

Certo*, (ser'tō)—Trade name for fruit pectin used in making jams and jellies. Certo jams require very short boiling periods, therefore retain the piquant fresh-fruit flavor. They also produce greater yield than jams made by the old-fashioned, long-boiling methods.

Cervelat, (ser̆ ve lät')—Like salami, but mildly seasoned.

Cerises, F. f. pl. (srēēz)—Cherries.

Cervelle, F. f. (ser̆ vĕl')—Brains.

Chablis*, F. (shä blee')—Very dry white wine originally from the Chablis region of France Now, type is also produced in U. S.

Chambertin

Chambertin*, F. (shăm ber tăn′)–Red Burgundy wine.

Champagne*, F. (shăm pain′)–Sparkling or effervescent pale or greenish-yellow wine regarded as a symbol of luxury living. Originally from the Champagne Districts of France. Much is still imported. Excellent American champagne is also available. Pink champagne has recently been highly promoted as a party drink. Also called "The Bubbly" by sophisticated party-givers.

Champagne Cocktail–Champagne seasoned with sugar, lemon peel and a dash of bitters. Simple syrup is preferable because when sugar is added to sparkling wines and stirred, the liquid tends to "boil over."

Champagne Cup–Drink made of champagne, liqueurs, and brandy. Decorated with fresh fruit.

Champignon, F. (shăm pē nyŏn′)–Mushrooms.

Chantilly Cream, F. (shăn tē yēē′)–Dessert of vanilla whipped cream, used as topping for puddings, etc.

Chantilly Sauce, F.–White sauce made by blending cold mayonnaise or hot Hollandaise with whipped cream. Named after the town of Chantilly in northern France.

Chapon, F. m. (shă pŏn′)–Capon. This term is also used to mean the heel of French bread rubbed with fresh garlic and put in the bottom of a salad bowl to impart a soupcon (little bit of) flavor.

Chard, Swiss–A kind of beet grown only for its stalks and leaves (usually green). Fresh leaves may be cut up in salads, or cooked like spinach. Now available as rhubarb chard with glowing red stalks. Prized by flower arrangers for striking floral effects.

Charlotte, F. f. (shär lōt)–Sweet dessert similar to Cabinet Pudding. Slices of stale bread alternate with sweetened stewed tart apples (mashed), sugar, nutmeg, butter and chopped almonds. Baked and served hot with fruit syrup or cream.

Charred oak casks–Used to age distilled spirits (four years required by law; 8-12 years for premium brands and 20 years or more for superior brands or grades). It's the inside of each cask that's charred. The charcoal absorbs impurities and produces a mellowing, smoothening effect on the liquor. It also produces the amber color characteristic of good whiskeys.

Chartreuse* verte or jaune, F. (shär trūse′vĕrt or shōn)–Green or yellow liqueur made originally by the Carthusian monks.

Chasse*, F. (shäss)–Brand of liqueur served after coffee.

Chasseur Sauce, F. (shä sur′)–Rich brown game sauce containing tomato paste, mushrooms and seasonings. Potage: game soup.

Chateaubriand, F. (shä tō brēē yŏn′)–Thick tenderloin steak.

Chateaubriand Sauce, F.–Made with fat, lemon juice, salt and pepper, minced parsley and Spanish Sauce.

Chateaubriant Espagnole Sauce, S. (ĕs pä nyōl′)–Spanish Sauce: minced lean raw ham, chopped celery and carrots, minced onions, flour, fat, soup stock and tomato juice.

Chateau Batailley*, F. (shä tō bä tǐyē′)–Bordeaux Claret from a celebrated wine-growing region.

Chateau Belgrave*, F. (bĕl gräv)–Bordeaux Claret from the Haut-Médoc region.

Chateau Haut Brion*, F. (ō brē yŏn′)–Bordeaux wine produced on the estate of Clarence Dillon, former American ambassador to France and later France's ambassador to the United States. Said to be "the finest" of its kind.

Chateau Lafite*, F. (lä fēēt′)–A fine Bordeaux Claret which Hugh Johnson, in his excellent book, titled "Wine," calls the "most beautiful of the three" produced by the two great vineyards of the Rothschild family. Lafite's vineyards cover 153 acres of the 300-acre estate, but only the best of their wine in any year is sold as Chateau Lafite.

Chateau Latour*, F. (lä tōōr′)–A "stylish" wine which is more masculine than Lafite, according to Johnson, who adds: "It has the reputation above all chateaux for consistency." Also produced by vineyards owned by the Rothschild family.

Chateau Latour Blanche,.F.–White Bordeaux Claret from a 200-year old vineyard in Pauillac, the finest and most famous of the Bordeaux communes.

Chateau Margaux*, F. (mär gō′)–Light, smooth Bordeaux Claret said to have ravishing scent. Comes from the Chateau Margaux in the town of the same name located in the superlative commune of the Medoc. A first-growth superior wine.

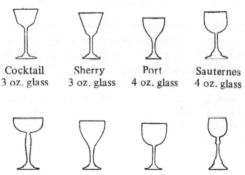

| Cocktail | Sherry | Port | Sauternes |
| 3 oz. glass | 3 oz. glass | 4 oz. glass | 4 oz. glass |

| Champagne | Burgundy | Claret | Rhine Wine |
| 5 to 6 oz. glass | 4 oz. glass | 4 oz. glass | 3 oz. glass |

Chateau Mouton-Rothschild*, F. (moo tŏn)—Strong, long-lasting, flavorful Bordeaux Claret from the estate of Baron Phillippe de Rothschild in the famous Pauillac commune of Bordeaux. Each label bears the total production of that vintage, how many bottles, magnums, double magnums, etc. A treasure among Bordeaux wines!

Chateau Pape Clement*, F. (klā mŏn′)—Chateau whose vineyards were first planted by the Bishop of Bordeaux in the 14th century. When he became Pope, he transferred papal headquarters to Avignon rather than forego the fine wine his vineyards yielded.

Chateau St. Emilion*, F. (ĕm ē yŏn′)—Full, savory, strong Bordeaux Claret from the largest wine-producing vineyards in Bordeaux. Hill-wines are known as Cotes-St. Emilion; those grown on gravelly flatlands are Graves-St. Emilion.

Chateau Yquem*, F. (ē kĕm′)—Rich, fresh, creamy Sauterne from the southernmost area of Bordeaux. Made with loving care. Only place where all the wine-producing machinery is made of wood (even intricate moving parts) so that no metal touches the wine. A wine to sip and enjoy, says Johnson.

Chaud, F. m. (shō) or Chaude, F. f. (sh ōd)—Hot.

Chaud-Froid Sauce, F. (shō frwä′)—White, brown or yellow sauces. White: gelatin soaked in cold water and added to a cup of hot Velouté Sauce. Strained and cooled, it is used to coat cold meats. Brown: like Velouté but made with brown roux and brown stock. Yellow: beaten yolks of two eggs are added to white chaud-froid before it is removed from the fire.

Cheese Bleu, F. (blue)—Looks like Roquefort, but is made of cows' milk instead of sheep's milk. Danish Blue Cheese is a type.

Cheese, brick—American-made. Stronger and sharper than Cheddar.

Cheese, Cheddar—Hard, smooth, yellow domestic cheese. Excellent for fondues and rarebits.

Cheese fondue (fŏn doo′)—Cheese, bread crumbs, scalded milk, butter, egg yolks, beaten egg whites, salt. Baked until firm. Similar to soufflé. All ingredients except egg whites are blended and cooked into a smooth, creamy sauce. Beaten egg whites are folded in last to give lightness.

Cheese, Gouda (goo′ dä)—Dutch cheese made of cows' milk and shaped like a flattened ball, covered with red waxy coating to prevent mold. Mild and smooth-textured without holes.

Cheese, Muenster, G. (minster)—Soft mild cheese originally from Germany. Now also American-made.

Cheese, Oka, Canadian—Shaped like a disc. Similar to brick cheese but stronger.

Cheese Pineapple—American Cheddar cooked hard and molded into pineapple shape.

Cheese, Processed—Blend of new and aged cheeses, shredded and pasteurized.

Cheese Puffs—Batter of flour, cheese, eggs, milk, and seasoning. Deep fat fried.

Cheese, Sage—American cheese made of cows' milk seasoned with minced sage (an herb).

Cheese Straws, Cheese Sticks—Crisp pastry sticks, savories, appetizers.

Cheese, Swiss—Also known as Gruyere, Emmenthal, Sweitzer or Switzerland Cheese. Evenly distributed large holes. Imported Swiss is yellow; American Swiss is white. Used for sandwiches alone or combined with ham or bologna. Served as dessert with pie or crackers and coffee. Now also packed in small wedges without rind and without holes.

Chef, F. (shĕf)—Head cook.

Chef de range, F. (shĕf dē ränzh)—Dining room or restaurant captain.

Chef's Salad—Entrée-type salad usually made of hard-cooked eggs, asparagus, lettuce, tomatoes, cress, chicory, green peppers, and seasoned with garlic and choice of salad dressings. May also be made of endive, romaine, cream cheese, grapefruit, pineapple, olives and pimiento. Shredded ham, tongue or bologna may be added on top of the vegetable combination.

Chemise, F. (shĕmeēs')—With skins, as potatoes boiled in their jackets or skins.

Cherry Brandy—Cherry Cordial.

Cherry Heering, D. (hĕrring)—Fine cherry liqueur from Denmark.

Cherry Tomatoes—Small red or yellow tomatoes, the size of a cherry or plum. Burpee now has the plum-size called "Small Fry." Red. Colorful garnish.

Chervil—Plant of the carrot family whose leaves are used for flavoring salads, soups, etc. See Fines Herbes.

Cheshire Cheese—Hard English cheese from cows' milk. Yellow.

Chevalier, à la, F. (shā väl'yē)—Usually food dipped in batter, fried and served with cream sauce.

Chevreuil, F. m. (sh ĕ vroy')—Venison.

Chianti, I. (kēy än'tĭ)—Red wine from Italy. Tart.

Chicken, broiler—8 to 12 weeks old; weighing less than 2½ pounds. Raised commercially in special scientifically-designed coops which have wire mesh floors raised above the ground to make running around impossible. Keeps meat tender. It's possible to buy large quantities of broilers of identical size, as needed for portion control in serving banquets.

Chicken, cocks—Mature male birds. Dark tough flesh.

Chicken Cutlets, à la Boyar—Chopped chicken cutlet served with rice, wine and mushroom sauce.

Chicken-fried Steak

Chicken-fried Steak—Steak dipped in flour, seasoning, and pan-fried or smothered.

Chicken, fryers—14-20 weeks old, weighing 2½ to 3½ pounds each.

Chicken Gumbo Soup—Chicken, pork, okra, tomatoes, cream, rice and seasoning.

Chicken Halibut—Young halibut weighing from 2 to 10 pounds each.

Chicken Livers à la Russe, R.—Chicken livers creamed au gratin, served en casserole.

Chicken Lobsters—Young lobsters weighing about a pound each.

Chicken Maryland—Disjointed young chickens seasoned, then dipped in flour, beaten eggs. Baked in oven or fried in deep fat. Served with gravy made from chicken stock and accompanied by corn fritters or bacon.

Chicken, roasters—5 to 9 months old. Over 3½ lb.

Chicken, slips—Incompletely caponized male birds, over 4 lbs.

Chicken, stags—Male birds older than roasters. Dark flesh.

Chicken Supreme—Breast of chicken sautéed. Served with rice and champagne sauce.

Chicken Tetrazzini—Chicken or turkey cut in large pieces, combined with medium cream sauce, or Mornay Sauce, sautéed mushrooms, cooked spaghetti, and dry sherry. Baked in shallow casserole at 350°F. May be covered with Parmesan cheese. Toasted almonds in place of mushrooms, optional. Named after the famous opera singer, Mme. Tetrazzini.

Chicory—Green leaves for salad. Roots roasted and ground fine to strengthen coffee.

Chiffon Pie—Fluffy pie filling of gelatin, egg yolks, sugar and beaten egg whites. May be flavored with lemon juice or cooked pumpkin pulp, etc.

Chiffonade, F. (shee fō näd')—Shredded lettuce and herbs used for soups and salads. Salad: cabbage, celery, chopped egg, beets or tomatoes, cress and lettuce. Salad Dressing: French Dressing with onions (minced), egg, parsley, and red peppers.

Chili con Carné, S. (chee lee kön kär'nā)—Beef (lean) cut in cubes, cubed beef suet, olive oil, minced onions, oregano, paprika, salt and pepper, chili powder, and hot water. Cook until tender. Serve with baked beans, rice or lima beans; or add red kidney beans to the meat before simmering. Hot Mexican dish.

Chili Peppers—Small. Red hot. Used in pickling, or dried and ground for seasoning.

Chili Powder—Made from dried Mexican peppers. Used in Chili con Carné.

Chili Sauce—Condiment made of tomatoes, chili peppers, vinegar and seasonings. More spicy than ketchup.

Chinese Cabbage—Long, green, lettuce-like head. Also called Celery Cabbage.

Chinook Salmon—Alaskan salmon of fine texture, deep pink color and excellent flavor. Rich in oil. Delicious when broiled. May weigh from 20 to 80 pounds.

Chipolata, à la (chee pō lä'tä)—Poultry with forcemeat, onions, turnips, mushrooms and chestnuts.

Chitterlings—Southern dish of small intestines of swine. Boiled and well seasoned, then cut in small pieces and rolled in egg and crumbs or flour and deep-fat fried.

Chives—Plant of onion family, with slender hollow stems or leaves. Used minced fine to give flavor to soups, stews, vegetables and salads.

Chopping—Cutting food into small pieces with a knife, cleaver, or other cutting instrument.

Chop Suey, C. (soo'e)—Chinese stew which may be made of chicken, pork, shrimp, or whatever. Added are: bamboo sprouts, onions, rice and perhaps water chestnuts.

Chou, F. m. sg. (shoo)—Cabbage, Choux de Bruxelles (shoos dě broo' sell)—Brussels sprouts.

Choucroutte Garni, F. (shoo croot gär nee')—Sauerkraut with ham, bacon, sausages, onions, juniper berries, boiled potatoes. See Allemande.

Choufleur, Choux-fleurs, F. (shoo fler')—Cauliflower.

Chou Rouge, F. (shoo roozh')—Red cabbage.

Choux à la Crême, F.—Pastry. Cream puffs.

Choux Farci, F. (shoo fär'see)—Cabbage leaves stuffed with ground meat and rice. Usually served with Hungarian Sauce.

Choux Pastry, F. Pâté à choux (pä tā ä shoo')—Pastry used for éclairs, cream puffs, etc. See Pâté à choux.

Choux Raves, F. (shoo räv')—Kohlrabi, a kind of cabbage with bulbous end which resembles a turnip. May be eaten raw or cooked.

Chow Chow—Relish made of green tomatoes, onions, peppers, celery, seasonings, etc.

Chowder—Thick soup of clams, oysters, or fish. New England style: with milk, creamy. Manhattan style: with tomatoes.

Chow Mein, C. (chow main')—Chinese dish of bean sprouts, celery, mushrooms, oil, almonds, and any meat: beef, pork, chicken, or shrimp. Served over crisp fried noodles. May be purchased in the frozen food section of grocery stores. Fried noodles available in cans.

Chutney Relish, sweet and highly seasoned, made of chopped vegetables and/or fruits. Served with hot or cold meats, sausages, stews or curries.

27

Cider

Cider—Juice pressed from apples. Used as a beverage; for making vinegar; or fermented and distilled into Apple Jack or Apple Brandy.

Cinnamon—Aromatic inner bark of tree or shrub of the laurel family, grown in East Indies. Used as bark in pickling and spiced wine drinks. Ground, it's fine with applesauce, pineapple, pies, tarts, etc.

Cinnamon Toast—Hot toast spread with butter, sugar and sprinkled with cinnamon. Good tea-time snack.

Citron—Yellow thick-skinned fruit resembling lime or lemon but larger and less acid. Semi-tropical. Candied rind is used as a confection, in fruit cake, etc.

Clams—Common American shellfish. "Little Necks" are hard-shelled, round "Quahaugs" popular in the East. Most tender when small and young. Must be served when fresh. Larger ones are used for broths and chowders. Soft-shelled clams are long and have distensible necks. Razor clams, grown in the tide flats of Puget Sound on the Pacific Coast, are much larger. Usually minced. Uses: served raw on the halfshell; broiled; fried; scalloped; mixed with other seafood in Newburgs; included in seafood platters; stewed; steamed; ground and made into chowders.

Claret—Red table wines. Many trade-name brands.

Clarifying fat—Drippings and fat from tried-out scraps allowed to harden. Removed from container with sediment that settled in the bottom of the cake scraped off and discarded. Hot water (boiling) poured over the remainder melts the cake enough to let more sediment settle to the bottom. Strained through cheesecloth placed over a strainer. When cooled, the solid cake is removed from the liquid. Process may need to be repeated to get a cake of clean fat.

Clover Club Cocktail—Gin, raspberry syrup, lemon juice, sugar, and egg white. Shaken over ice to froth.

Cloves—Pungent fragrant spice from the dried buds of an evergreen tree native to East Indies. Whole cloves used in pickling and studding ham prior to baking. Powdered cloves used largely in baking.

Club House Sandwich—Three decker, made by combining chicken, bacon, lettuce in layers between 3 slices of bread and garnishing with tomato and/or olives.

Club Soda—Carbonated distilled water with added minerals.

Cloche, sous, F. (soo clōsh')—Under bell or domed cover.

Club Steak—Small beefsteak cut from the loin tip.

28

Coating—Dipping food into seasoned flour or crumbs; or alternately in egg mixture and flour or crumbs. Used before frying or baking chops or chicken.

Cobbler—Baked dessert of flaky crust with filling of apples, berries, peaches, or plums, etc.

Cobbler—Drink containing liquor, sugar, mint and sliced fruit.

Cock-a-leekie—Scotch soup of chicken stock and leeks.

Cocktail Mixed drink of spirits, bitters, sugar and flavoring, served iced. Usually shaken over ice in a cocktail shaker and strained into a stemmed glass. Term also applies to tasty food served in a glass as a first course (fruit, oysters, sea-food).

Cocoa—Chocolate from which some of the oil has been removed.

Coconut—Hard-shelled fruit of the coco palm. Coconut milk is used in some exotic mixed drinks. Coconut meat may be used fresh or dried; usually shredded, as topping for desserts.

Cocotte, F.—Small earthen cooking ware.

Codfish Important food fish found in salt waters of the North Atlantic, as off the banks of Newfoundland and the coast of Norway. May be served fresh or salted-dried as a base for creamed dishes.

Coddled Eggs, also spelled "caudled"—Cooked below the boiling point, after water has stopped boiling. Soft boiled.

Coddling—Cooking below the boiling point, gently. Eggs so-cooked are said to be more tender.

Coeurs, F. m. pl. (ker)—Hearts (as of artichokes), core.

Coffee—An aromatic drink made from the roasted and ground berries of a plant grown in many parts of the world. Its taste may be judged from the color of the roasted bean: light = mildest; medium = stronger; dark = strongest, but may be bitter. Powdered or pulverized coffee produces the greatest yield but requires special equipment. May be served black, with hot milk or sweet cream. Cream substitutes which are non-dairy products with long-keeping qualities are used in many commercial establishments—especially kosher.

Coffee, Drip—Pouring boiling water over finely-ground coffee all at one time. Usually requires a fine-meshed strainer or filter for making clear beverage. Commonly used commercial method.

Coffee, Percolated—Process of constantly syphoning boiling water over ground coffee.

Coffee, French—Strong, with about ¼ roasted chicory.

Coffee Imperial, R.—Hot coffee with Vodka.

Coffee, Turkish—Strong, thickish, sweet drink served in demi-tasse cups as a specialty. Made with finely pulverized coffee.

Cognac*, F. (kō nyăk′)—French brandy. See Brandy.

Cointreau

Cointreau*, F. (kwän trō′)–Trade name for orange cordial. Also called Triple Sec.

Colbert Sauce–Brown gravy seasoned with claret, shallots, butter, lemon juice.

Cole Slaw–Salad made of shredded cabbage; may be served with sour cream dressing, boiled dressing, or combined with other vegetables in aspics.

Cholesterol–Important fatty substance involved in vital functions of human blood and tissues. Over-abundance is said to induce hardening of arteries and arterio-sclerosis. Medical authorities say high-cholesterol diets tend to lead to formation of fatty deposits inside of veins and arteries, thereby narrowing blood-carrying channels and overworking the heart. In such cases, they recommend reduced intake of animal fats such as butter, cream, eggs, and fat meats. These so-called "saturated fats" are said to increase the cholesterol content of human blood. See saturated fats, also polyunsaturated fats.

Collins–Tall drinks of liquor, lemon or lime juice, sugar, seltzer, over ice. May be garnished with fruit slices and maraschino cherries. Liquor may be rum or gin.

Combination Salad–Mixed vegetables seasoned with choice of dressing: French, Italian, Mayonnaise or Thousand Island. Some patrons prefer Roquefort Dressing.

Compote–Stewed fruit usually served in a glass.

Commis de Rang, F. (commēē dĕ räng′)–Assistant waiter who also does bus boy service.

Condiments–Sauces used for seasoning, such as A-1, ketchup, Teri-Yaki, Worcestershire, Escoffier, Diable.

Condensed Milk–Sugar added in condensing process.

Confiture, F. f. (kŏn fēē tūre′)–Jam.

Conserves, F. f. pl. (kŏn serv′)–Preserves. Fruits and nuts cooked with sugar until thick.

Consommé, F. m. (kŏn sō mā′)–Clear broth. May be served plain or used in flavoring various dishes. Also is often served chilled or jellied, especially in summer.

Consommé Double Celestine–Clear soup with little pancakes floated on top.

Contrefilet, F. m. (kŏn trĕ fēē lāy′)–Boned sirloin.

Cooler–Tall drink similar to a Collins: liquor, fruit juice, seltzer, over ice.

Coquilles, F. f. pl. (kō kēē yē′)–Cockles. Scallops. Shell-shaped dishes. Also used to describe minced poultry or meat served on shells.

Corbeille, F. (kōr bāyēē′)–Fresh fruit served in a basket.

30

Cordial—Aromatized, sweetened spiritous liquor. Great variety of flavors and colors. Originally made from fresh fruit juices, sugar, flavorings and alcohol. See Liqueurs.

Cordon Bleu, F. (kōr dŏn ble̲′)—Famous French cooking school; recipe originating there; chef trained there.

Coriander Seeds—From a European carrot-family plant. Used in flavoring foods and liqueurs. Strong.

Corn—Also called Maize. Pilgrims learned about it from the American Indians. Now an important staple crop raised extensively in the U. S. Many varieties and uses. Lower in protein than wheat or oats, but rich in fat and oil.

Sweet corn, a "farm crop" is eaten when "green" or unripe. Boiled, it is served "on the cob" with butter. Canned or frozen kernels make green corn available all year.

Ripe corn, white or yellow, may be coarse-ground into hominy or grits. Fine-ground, it makes the very useful corn meal, a staple food in many areas.

Oil pressed from corn germ is used as a cooking fat, salad oil or for making margarine. Starchy portions of the kernel provide edible cornstarch, laundry starch, and dextrin (substitute for gum arabic in textile trades).

Corn meal may be boiled into mush, a breakfast cereal; baked into corn bread, muffins, spoon bread or pone; fried in deep fat as hush puppies. Steamed, it makes pudding, corn bread, and Mexican Tamales.

Corn syrup is used with pancakes or waffles, in baking or confectionery.

Fermented corn is the chief ingredient in Bourbon Whiskey, also called "Corn Whiskey," and as an ingredient in making other alcoholic beverages.

Corn Meal Dodger—Similar to dumplings.

Corn Meal Muffins—Mixture of corn meal and white flour, milk, eggs, shortening and baking powder.

Corn Pone—Southern favorite. Baked corn meal bread.

Cornucopia—Pastry roll (horn), filled with whipped cream or meringue and nuts. Or, for a party buffet, a large paper or plastic cornucopia filled with choice fruits spilling over onto the table. The cornucopia may also be carved out of ice and lighted from the back.

Cos—Salad green similar to Romaine lettuce.

Cotelette, F. f. sg. (kōt elĕt′)—Cutlet.

Cottage Cheese—Soft, white, fresh unripened cheese.

Cottage-fried Potatoes—Sliced or diced raw potatoes seasoned and fried with a brown crust.

Cottage Pudding

Cottage Pudding—Mixture of flour, egg, shortening, sugar, salt, milk and baking powder blended into a pouring batter. Baked in moderate oven (375° - 400°F.) Hot sauce over all.

Coupe, F. f. pl. (ko͞op)—Ice cream served in glasses with fruit and Chantilly Cream.

Coupe Jacques, F. f. sg. (ko͞op zhäk′)—Fruit salad with vanilla ice cream or sherbet served in a compote glass.

Court Bouillon—Fish Bouillon (fish stock). Whitefish heads and trimmings, cold water, peppercorns, cloves, bay leaf, carrots, celery, onions, boiled half the time needed for other stocks.

Couvert, F. m. sg. (ko͞o vair′)—Cover: table set-up for one person. Cover charge.

Cover Charge—Fixed fee for table service independent of the charge for food. Usually in night clubs or posh restaurants offering entertainment.

Crabs, Soft Shell—Crabs when they have just cast off their hard shells before they grow new and larger ones.

Craburgers—Crab meat, eggs, seasoning mixed to make small cakes which are fried to brown on each side. Served on biscuits.

Cracklings—Crisped salt pork after the fat has been rendered out.

Crawfish or Crayfish—Fresh water crustaceans of the lobster type.

Cream Cheese—Made from whole milk and cream. Soft, white, and smooth.

Creaming—Cooking term which means working one or more foods until soft and creamy, such as sugar and shortening as a base for making cakes.

Cream Puff—Pastry puff filled with whipped cream.

Cream Sauce—White Béchamel reduced with milk or cream. Usually made by blending flour and butter and cooking into a roux, then adding milk and cooking until smooth and creamy. Used as a base for many creamed dishes: chicken, turkey, sea-foods vegetables. Thin cream sauce is also a base for casserole dishes, such as Chicken à la King.

Crême, F. f. (kraim)—Cream.

Crême de Cacao*, F. (kraim de̱ kākā ō)—Chocolate cordial.

Crême de Cassis*, F. (kraim de̱ kä se͞e′)—Currant cordial.

Crême de Menthe*, F. (kraim de̱ mänth)—Liqueur flavored with mint, white or green.

Crême de Violette, F. (kraim de̱ vee ō lĕt′)—Sweet liqueur from Holland, vanilla and cocoa with oil of violets. Amethyst color.

Crême Fouettée, F. f. (kraim fo͞o ā tā′)—Whipped cream.

Crême Yvette, F. (kraim ye͞e vĕt′)—Sweet lavender-hued cordial.

Créole Goulash—Southern dish of kidney beans, bacon, tomatoes and cheese.

Créole Sauce, F. (kräōl')—Green peppers and tomatoes. Soup or fish à la Créole—same ingredients.

Créole Sweet Potatoes—Brown stock, caramel, nutmeg, celery salt added to peeled sweet potatoes or yams. Baked.

Crêpes, F. f. pl. (kräp)—Pancakes.

Crêpes Suzette, F.—Thin French pancakes served with a rich sauce. Sometimes served with flaming spirits.

Crêpinettes, F. f. pl. (krā pee nĕt')—Breaded grilled croquettes of meat, poultry or game. Garnished with vegetables.

Cress, watercress—Plant of the mustard family whose crisp green leaves are used in salads, party sandwiches, and garnishes. Grows wild along water courses; obtainable from greenhouses almost all year. Use young leaves; old ones get too peppery.

Cresson, F. m. (krā sŏn')—Watercress.

Crisping—To make salad greens firm and brittle in moderate heat followed by cold water. To chill in ice water.

Croissant, F. m. (krwä sän')—Crescent-shaped French roll.

Croquette, F. f. (krō kĕt')—Chopped or ground meat rolled in bread crumbs or corn meal and fried in a skillet, deep fat or oven-baked.

Croustade, F. f. pl. (krōō städ')—Baked forms or patty shells. Also hot patties filled with a meat or liver paste.

Croutons, F. m. pl. (krōō tŏn')—Diced fried bread floated on top of soups.

Cruller—Long, twisted doughnut.

Crumpet—English breakfast batter cake: made of milk, butter, eggs, flour.

Crustaceans—Shellfish (crabs, lobsters, shrimps, etc.)

Crustas—Drink served in a glass whose rim has been encrusted by dipping in powdered sugar. Liquor, fruit juice, sugar, sliced fruit and berries.

Cuba Libre—Long drink of rum, Coca Cola, lime juice.

Cubed or Cubing—Cutting in small cubes.

Cuisine, F. f. (kwee seen')—Style of cookery, as French, Spanish, Mexican, American.

Cuisinier, F. m., **Cuisiniere,** F. f. (kwee see nee ā) (air)—Cook.

Cuisses de Grenouilles Frites, F. (kwees'de grĕn ōō'ēē freet")—Fried frogs' legs.

Cuissot de Veau, F. m. (kwee sō de vō')—Kernel of veal.

Culinaire, F. (cū lĭn air)—Refers to the art of cooking.

Cumberland Salad Dressing—French Dressing with currant jelly.

Cumberland Sauce—Juice and peel of oranges and lemons with currant jelly and Port Wine.

Cumin, cummin—Seasoning used in curries.

Cups

Cups, pl.—Drinks made of cordials, liquors, wines, sugar, seltzer, sliced fruit or whole berries, mint. Usually served in large pitchers.

Curacao, F. (kūr'e sō")—Orange cordial.

Currants—Fresh: small berries with piquant flavor prized for jellies and conserves. Dried: small seedless raisins.

Cured—Dried or smoked: fish, meat, sausage.

Curries—Stews seasoned with curry powder. Originally from India.

Curry Powder—Blend of crushed or ground spices and aromatic seeds used to flavor soups and stews of lamb, chicken, pork, venison. Served with boiled rice, eggplant, and seasoned with table sauces or condiments. Origin: India.

Custard—Pudding made of eggs, milk, sugar, flavoring. Baked or boiled.

Cutlets de Voiaille—Russian way of preparing breaded breast of chicken. Fried. (Pronounced as in French, de voy eye).

Cutlets Marechal—Russian. Breast of chicken stuffed with mushrooms.

Cutlets Pojarsky—Russian variety of chicken and veal croquettes served with assorted vegetables.

Cutting in—Blending fat and flour with a knife until well mixed as for biscuits or pie crust. Flaky.

Cymling—Summer squash.

Cyrano—Clear chicken soup served with grated cheese.

Czarina Cocktail—Vodka, pineapple juice and bitters.

Toppings add interest to soup service; bits of cheese that float on top of cup of chicken soup introduce new flavor.

Dahl—East Indian dish of lentils, rice, onions, garlic and seasoning.

Daiquiri (dye′kēē rēē)—Cuban or Puerto Rican Rum.·

Daiquiri Cocktail—Daiquiri or light Bacardi Rum, lime juice, sugar, shaken over ice. Frozen Daiquiri, a showy concoction, resembles a scoop of sherbet in a cocktail glass.

Daiquiri, West Indian Style—Double size drink flavored with Maraschino Cordial.

Daisies (drinks)—Same as Crustas without encrusting the glass rim.

Dampfnudeln, G. (damf nōō′dĕln)—Sweet German dessert garnished with English cream sauce. See Nouilles à la Crême.

Damson Plums—Small, dark purplish plums, a little larger than Beach Plums, which make distinctive flavorful preserves.

Dandelion Greens—Edible leaves of a rampant-growing weed. May be cooked like spinach, cut up green and fresh in salads, or made like Dutch or wilted lettuce by tossing cleaned leaves in a skillet with bacon fat, salt, sugar, crisped bits of bacon, and lastly, sweet cream. Available cultivated.

Danish Apple Cake—Bread crumbs, cinnamon, sugar with alternate layers of sliced apples. Baked and served with a topping of whipped cream.

Dasheen—Potato-like vegetable from the South.

Dauphine, F. (dō fēēn′)—German-style pancake.

Deep Dish Pie—Fruit or meat pie baked in a deep dish or small casserole with crust on top only.

Déjeuner, F. n. (dā zhu nā)—Breakfast.

Delicatessen—Food specialties or delicacies which are ready to serve. Store which handles such foods.

Delmonico Potatoes—Creamed potatoes turned into a buttered baking dish and covered with buttered crumbs. Baked. Grated cheese topping optional. Baked only until cheese has melted.

Delmonico Salad—Herring, tongue, potatoes, apples, beets arranged on a bed of crisp lettuce and served with French Dressing. Garnished with watercress or parsley.

Delmonico Steak—Same as Club Steak. Boneless.

Demerara Rum*—A brand from British Guiana.

Demi, F. (dĕm′ē)—Half.

Demi Glacé, F. (dĕm ē gläsā′)—Ice cream.

Demi Sec, F. f. (dĕm ē sĕk′)—Half dry. Medium sweet, as wine.

Demi tasse, F. f. (dĕm ē täss′)—Small cup of coffee; after-dinner coffee. Literally, "half cup."

Denver Sandwich

Denver Sandwich—Similar to a Western Sandwich. Finely chopped, baked or boiled ham stirred into beaten egg, then fried. Garnished with lettuce and olives.

Dessert, F. m. (dā sair′)—Final course of the meal. Sweets, fruits, pastries, etc.

Dessertspoonful—Measure equalling ¼ oz.

Dessicated Eggs—Dried eggs, sometimes used in baking. May be purchased as whole eggs or whites and yolks separately. Long keeping quality.

Devilled Eggs—Hard-cooked eggs cut in half lengthwise. Mashed egg yolks are seasoned, then stuffed back into the whites. Often used as garnish for salads or added to hors d'oeuvres assortments.

Devil's Food Cake—Brown chocolate cake with fudge frosting or chocolate cream filling. For contrast, dark cakes are covered with white frosting.

Devilled—Highly seasoned, chopped or ground mixture, as of ham, oysters, clams, etc.

Devonshire Cream—Sweet cream cooked slowly in double-boiler until thick. Spooned over fresh berries or chilled in molds.

Diable, F. (dēē äbl)—Salad dressing made with wine or cider vinegar, chopped shallots, garlic, cayenne and minced parsley.

Diable Sauce*—Trade name for a bottled condiment used over meats, at table.

Diamond-back Terrapin—Small freshwater turtle with shell marked in prisms. Best in market. Great delicacy. Meat is usually diced and served in soup.

Diana Salad—Diced boiled potatoes and chicken seasoned with truffles.

Diced—Cut in small cubes. Neater and more appetizing than food cut into random shapes.

Dill—Herb of the carrot family. Young leaves: flavoring pickles and salads. Dried seeds: pickling, especially dill pickles (half-sour). Essential oil of dill is preferred by the food industry for dill pickles, spiced vinegar, condiment sauces and canned food specialties.

Dinde, F. f. (dănd)—Turkey hen.

Dindon, F. m. (dănd ŏn)—Turkey gobbler.

Dindonneau, F. (dănd e nō′)—Young turkey.

Diner, F. m. (dēē nā′)—Dinner.

Dinner—English term for the big meal of the day. Originally the noon meal; now the evening meal.

Diplomat Pudding—Molded Bavarian Cream with jelly or sauce similar to Cardinal.

Dobos Cake—Rich cake with nine thin layers, separated by chocolate spread or tart fruit jelly.

Doctor Cocktail—Swedish Punch with lime juice.

Dolmas—Oriental concoction of meat, rice, vegetables and spices.

Dotting—To put small pieces, as of butter, on top of foods prior to broiling or baking.

Doughnut—Round fried cakes (deep fat) with a hole in the center. Doughnut balls (cut-outs from the holes), fried, are dainty and equally good.

Doux, F. (duh)—Describes the sweetest wine or champagne.

Drambuie*, (dräm bōō′ēē)—Pale brown Scotch liqueur.

Drawn Butter Sauce—Yellow sauce made of melted butter mixed with flour, salt and a liquid.

Dredging—Coating with flour or bread crumbs.

Dredger—A large glass shaker containing sugar; used for sprinkling sugar over doughnuts or unfrosted cakes.

Dress—Culinary term meaning to trim, clean, etc.

Drippings—Fat and juice which drip from roasting meats. Valuable for basting meat during roasting process to prevent it from drying out or burning. Flavorful base for gravies.

Dry—Not sweet. A dry beverage contains a low percentage of sugar.

Dubonnet*, F. (dōō″bō nā′)—French aromatized tonic wine. A good aperitif. Now also made in California under license.

Dubonnet Cocktail—Gin, Dubonnet, orange bitters.

Dubonnet Fizz—Dubonnet, cherry brandy, juice of lemon and orange, seltzer, ice. Tall drink.

Duchesse, à la, F. (du shĕss′)—Sauce: Bechamel with mushrooms and ham. Potage: thick poultry soup with asparagus tips and truffles. Meats: with Duchess potatoes and braised lettuce. Fish: with oyster sauce.

Duchess Potatoes—Mashed with eggs; squeezed through a pastry tube, to decorate a service platter.

Duck—Domestic water fowl, raised commercially (as in Long Island) for table service. Good as ducklings or full grown. Available in equal-size birds, valuable for portion control as in banquet service. Usually roasted. Delicious with orange sauce.

Du Jour, F. (dōō zhōōr) Food ready to serve that day.

Dunking—Dipping into liquid, like dunking doughnuts in coffee.

Duo Carolus*—Sparkling citrus-flavored wine with a flavor resembling champagne.

Dusting—Sprinkling with flour or fine sugar.

Dutch Cheese—Usually Edam. See Edam.

Dutch Cocoa—Chemically-treated cocoa made almost as dark as chocolate.

37

Dutch Oven

Dutch Oven—Frying pan or spider with cover.

Dutch Potatoes—Baked with frankfurter inserted in a tunnel or hole scooped lengthwise through each potato.

Dutch Slaw—Finely shredded cabbage, steamed and served with dressing of egg, vinegar, sugar, salt and other seasonings desired.

Braise pan (Braisiere) may be round or oblong. It should have a high border and tightly-fitting cover. Purpose of braising meats: to cook tough pieces of meat to tenderness and to produce tasty sauce.

Eau, F. f. (ōh)—Water.

Eau de Vie, F. f. (ōh de vēē′)—Brandy, spirits, whiskey, etc. Literally means,"water of life."

Eaux Minerals, F. (ō mǐ nā·räl′)—Mineral waters.

Eclairs, F. m. pl. (ā klair′)—French pastry filled with whipped cream or custard.

Ecossaise, F. (ĕkō sāys)—Scottish style.

Ecrevisses, F. f. pl. (ā kre vees′)—Crawfish, crayfish, (f. w. f.).

Edam* (ē däm)—Trade name for a Dutch cheese formed in a flattened ball and coated with red waxy substance to prevent mold. Compact texture. Mild.

Eel, Conger—Long, scale-less, snake-like fish living in either fresh or salt water. Broiled, boiled, fried; served with sauce, in pies, stuffed or baked. A menu specialty.

Egri Bikaver*—Red Hungarian wine.

Eggplant—Large, pear-shaped vegetable covered with a smooth purplish skin. Prepared by dipping slices in flour or eggs and crumbs, then fried. May be escalloped with tomatoes, in Spanish or Mexican style.

Eggs, Admiral—with creamed chicken and truffles.

Eggs Africaine—Poached and served with peppers and rice, covered with Sauce Colbert.

Eggs à la Goldenrod—Chopped or sliced hard-cooked eggs in cream sauce, served over toast. Hard-cooked yolks, pressed through a wire sieve, are sprinkled on top. A sprig of watercress or parsley accents contrast between golden topping and sharp green garnish.

Eggs Anglaise, F. (ŏn glāze′)—Eggs with bacon.

Eggs, a la Bercy, F. (ber′see)—With pork sausage, tomato sauce, onions, cream and bread crumbs. Baked.

Eggs à la Créole, F.—Hard-cooked yolks mixed with Créole garniture, baked and served with rice.

Eggs à la Espagnole, F. (ĕs pä nyŏl′)—Hard-cooked eggs with rice and Espagnole Sauce (characterized by addition of onions and tomatoes). May also be served as an omelet, fried with Spanish Sauce folded in or poured over.

Eggs au Fondu, F. (ō fŏn dū′)—Poached eggs on toast, covered with Welsh rarebit.

Eggs à la Mornay, F. (mōr′nāy)—Poached on toast; covered with cream sauce and grated cheese. Placed under broiler just long enough to melt cheese.

Eggs à la Suisse

Eggs à la Suisse, F. (sweess)–Baked with cheese.

Eggs Argenteuil, F. (är zhĕn tēēl')–Poached eggs served with fresh asparagus tips and cream sauce.

Eggs à la Turque, F. (turk)–Shirred eggs with broiled chicken livers, brown gravy and topped with truffles.

Eggs Beaujolais, F. (bō zhō lāy')–Poached on toast and covered with Sauce Colbert. See Colbert Sauce.

Eggs Bénédict, F. (bā'nā dĭck)–Poached egg served on toasted English muffin that's covered with tongue or devilled ham spread. Garnished with hot Hollandaise Sauce.

Eggs Bercy, F. (Ber'see)–Shirred eggs with crumbled sausage (fried or broiled) and topped with tomato sauce.

Eggs Bonne Femme, F. (bŏn fĕm)–Bacon and eggs cooked in oven, seasoned and garnished (as with leeks, carrots, onions, etc.).

Eggs Bretonne, F. (brā tŏn')–With Madeira wine, brown sauce and puree of onions.

Eggs, candled–Eggs examined in front of electric light to determine freshness and quality. If yolk is intact and white albumin is clear, the egg may be judged to be fresh.

Eggs Celestine, F. (sĕll ĕs'tēēn″)–Like Eggs Benedict except with cheese sauce.

Eggs Cocotte, F. (kō kōt')–Cooked in sweet cream. See Shirred Eggs.

Eggs Chateaubriand, F. (shä tō'brēē än')–Poached eggs served on toast which has been covered with foie gras; the whole smothered in tomato sauce.

Eggs du Barry, F.–Hard-cooked eggs in white sauce garnished with anchovies and chives.

Eggs, Farci, F. (fär sēē')–Hard-cooked eggs shelled and cut in half crosswise. Cut small slice from end of each half so they will stand up in a pan. Mash yolks, season and heap into hollows of whites. Bake in shallow pan for six minutes. Serve on hot dish. Cover with any preferred sauce.

Eggs Florentine, I,–Poached, served on a bed of creamed, boiled spinach and browned in the oven.

Eggs Foo Yong–Chinese dish of eggs, bean sprouts, and subgum (mushrooms), served with fried almonds and rice. May be made with chicken, shrimp, etc.

Eggs frizzled–New England favorite. Fry broken bits of chipped beef. Add cream sauce. Pour over toast. Top with poached egg. Or pour beaten eggs over frizzled chipped beef and cook slowly like an omelet.

Eggs Mirabeau, F. (mē'rä bō″)–Stuffed eggs baked in cream sauce.

Eggnog–A drink especially favored for yuletide festivities. Yolks are beaten with sugar until thick. Bourbon and brandy, stirred in thoroughly, "cook" the eggs. Add milk and heavy cream. Vanilla ice cream is optional. Fold in stiffly-beaten egg whites. Chill. Sprinkle with nutmeg. Serve. Some fine restaurants greet patrons who come for Thanksgiving or Christmas dinner with a cup of eggnog "on the house."

Egg Noodles—Noodles in which eggs have been added to flour and water. Richer. Tastier.

Eggs Oriental, or Orientale (ō rē ĕn täl′)–Poached eggs served on slice of fresh tomato and covered with Hollandaise Sauce. Garnish with cucumber slices.

Eggs Ranchero (Texas special)—Scrambled with cheese, chopped onions, pepper and fried in butter.

Eggs Rivoli, F. (rēē′vō lēē)—On top of hash (roast beef, chicken, turkey or whatever), covered with white sauce, then baked.

Eggs Suzette—Baked potato scooped out and filled with egg, then baked.

Eggs Talleyrand—Poached eggs served on artichoke heart with foie gras and sauce.

Emincé, F. (ā″män sā′)—Minced, chopped fine or sliced very thin.

Emincé de Boeuf, F. (ā män sā de buff)—Thin slices of beef.

En brochette, F. (ŏn brō shĕt′)—Broiled on a skewer.

En Caraffe, F. (ŏn kä rähf′)—Wine from a cask served in a wine pitcher.

en Casserole, F. (on căss e rōle′)—Food served in the same dish in which it was baked.

Enchiladas—Mexican tortillas covered with sauce of grated cheese, highly seasoned.

en Chemise, F. (shĕm ēēz′)—Potatoes boiled in their skins.

en Coquille, F. (ŏn kō kēēl′)—In the shell.

Endive, F. (ŏn dēēv′)—Salad green like chicory. English term is pronounced "en dive." (ĕn dīv)

English Lamb Chop—Two inches thick, broiled.

English Steak and Kidney Pie—Cubed steak and kidneys sautéed with browned onions, seasoned and cooked until tender. Add thickening and pour into casserole. Top with pie crust or baking powder biscuits. Bake. Red wine may be added to gravy.

English Monkey—Well-seasoned cheese sauce served on toast or crackers.

en Pension, F. (ŏn pän′sĭŏn)—"American plan," room and board, i.e., meals included in price for lodging.

en Tasse, F. (ŏn täss′)—Served in a cup, as soup.

Entrecote, F. (on′tre kot)—Steak cut from between the ribs. Sirloin.

Entrée, F. (ŏn trā′)—Originally, food served between heavy courses. Now generally refers to the main dish.

41

Entremets

Entremets, F. m. sg. (ŏn trẹ māy′)—A sweet, such as dessert. Usually the last dish.

Enzyme—Organic substance, such as pepsin; a digestive juice.

Épaule, F. f. (ā pōl)—Shoulder.

Eperlans, F. m. pl. (ā pair′län)—Smelts. (s. w. f.).

Épicé, F. (ā pee sä′)—Highly spiced.

Épice, F. (ā′peess)—Spice.

Epicure—Lover of good food and wine. One who knows.

Epicurean Salad—Combination of watercress, celery, onions, green peppers, radishes, with Mayonnaise Dressing.

Epinards, F. m. pl. (ā′pee när)—Spinach. See Spinach.

Escalop—Sea mollusk, better known as "scallop." To bake with crumbs in a cream sauce.

Escallope de Veau a la Viennoise (dẹ vō ä lä vän wäz)—Wiener or Viener Schnitzel.

Escargots, F. m. pl. (ĕs″kär gō′)—Snails.

Escarole—A kind of endive whose leaves are used in salads.

Escoffier, F. (ĕs kō′fee ā)—Name of a famous French chef.

Escoffier Sauce*—Trade name of an epicurean condiment.

Espadon, F. m. (ĕs′pä dōn″)—Swordfish. (s. w. f.)

Espagnole, F. (ĕs pä nyōl′)—Spanish Sauce, Spanish Cream, Spanish Rice, Spanish Omelet.

Espagnole Salad, F.—Romaine, avocado, persimmons, lettuce.

Essence—Juice from food.

Essential Oils—Oils extracted from plants, as peppermint extract. Useful for flavoring foods.

Est-Est-Est—Italian sparkling wine, sweet and white.

Estate Bottling—System of producing and bottling wines in France and Germany. Indicates that grapes were grown and wine made and bottled "on the premises" under the supervision of the owners. Nearest thing to brand names as an indication of quality. See Chateau wines.

Esturgeon, F. (ĕs′tur zhŏn″)—Sturgeon.

Etouffé, F. (ā tōō fā′)—Stewed food.

Etuvée, F. (ā tōō vā′)—Stewed meat.

Evaporated Milk—Condensed without the addition of sugar.

Evian, F. (ā′vee än)—Mineral water from France.

Ewes—Female sheep over 20 months old, weighing from 60 to 100 lb. per carcass.

Faisan, F. m. (fā sän′)—Pheasant.

Family Flour—Blended all-purpose flour, combining hard and soft wheats.

Farce, F. (färs)—Stuffing.

Farci, -e, F. (fär see′)—Stuffed.

Farina—Coarsely-ground inner portion of hard Spring Wheat. Boiled as a hot breakfast food. Fried leftovers take the place of potatoes. May be used in puddings or to make gruel.

Fat—Term applied to solid and liquid edible fats; lard, cooking oils, salad oils, butter, shortening, hydrogenized vegetable oils, etc.

Fennel—Vegetable resembling celery, except with bulbous stalk. Served chilled like celery. Has slight anise flavor. Origin: Italy—finocchio.

Fennel Seed—Used to flavor breads, pastries, fruit pies, sauces, sausage, canned foods and condiments. Continental.

Fernet Branca*, I. (fair′nā brän″kä)—Trade name for a bitters concoction used in cocktails.

Feuilletage, F. (few ee tazh)—Puff paste.

Fifth—Size of a liquor bottle, containing 25.6 oz. in contrast to a quart which holds 32 oz. Used extensively for distilled spirits.

Figaro Sauce—Tomato purée, mayonnaise and seasonings.

Figues, F. (feeg)—Figs.

Filbert—Round nut. Cultivated variety is the Hazelnut. Distinctive flavor. Tasty addition to mixed nuts.

Filet, F. m. (fee lā′)—Tenderloin of beef, mutton, veal, or pork without the bone. Boned fish are also called filets.

Filet Chateaubriand—Russian specialty: extra thick Filet Mignon baked in oven; served with truffles and champignons (mushrooms).

Filet Mignon, F. m. (fee lā mee nyŏn′)—Tenderloin of beef. Choicest cut.

Filet of Sole Marguery, F. (mär′gä ree″)—Poached sole or flounder served with a specialty sauce of mussels, shrimps, fish or chicken stock, egg yolks, butter and seasoning.

Financiere, à la, F. (fee nän see air′)—Sauce: Brown sauce with truffles and mushrooms. Garnish: Mushrooms, olives, cucumbers. Soup: Goose liver cream soup with croutons.

Fine Champagne, F. (feen shäm pain′)—French for Cognac, brandy.

Fines Herbes, F. (feen′airb)—Mixture of chopped or minced chives, garlic, parsley, tarragon. Used for seasoning sauces and stews. See Fines Herbes Sauce.

Fines Herbes Sauce

Fines Herbes Sauce, F. (feens'airb)—White or brown sauce flavored with white wine, parsley, and herb mixture. See Fines Herbes.

Finan Haddie—Smoked haddock. (s. w. f.).

Finocchio (or fennel), I. (fee no'ke o)—Fragrant vegetable of the celery family. See Fennel.

Fish and Chips—Traditional English favorite consisting of white fish, like haddock, fried in deep fat and served with potato chips.

Fish balls—Scandinavian dish of haddock, fish stock, cereals and flour, made into small patties and fried.

Fish pie—Usually made with cod, mashed potatoes, suet, bread crumbs, milk, butter, eggs. Cooked and served in a casserole.

Fizzes, pl.—Tall drinks, seltzer served cold. Liquor, lemon juice, sugar, lemon peel, ice. Experienced bartenders make a real production out of stimulating the "fizz" by shaking the drink briskly.

Flageolets, F. pl. (flä zhēō lĕt)—Green Kidney beans.

Flamande, à la (flä mänd')—Consomme or Potage: with Brussels Sprouts. Sauce: Butter sauce with mustard, parsley, lemon juice. Fish: poached in wine and butter, served with Fines Herbes and slices of lemon. Meats: with Brussels Sprouts, carrots and turnips.

Flambé, -e, F. (fläm bā')—Any meat dish or dessert served while in flame from the lighted spirits poured over it. Sophisticated service.

Flambées, F. pl.—Drinks similar to Blazers, served while flaming. Dramatic but could be dangerous. Check your insurance policy. Don't try this in fine thin, crystal glasses (as for pousse cafe), if you value them.

Flank—Hindquarters of beef, below sirloin.

Flannel Cakes—Griddle cakes of flour, baking powder, eggs, butter, mace.

Flapjacks—Pancakes. See Flannel Cakes.

Flash freezing—An improved process for preserving food, used by the food industry. Temperature drops very fast to very low point for a limited time, then is raised to customary levels for frozen foods. Fast freezing causes liquids in foods to form fine-grained crystals which do not break tissues or allow flavor to ooze out, hence retains desirable flavor.

Fleurette Sauce, F. (flur ĕt')—Butter, chopped chives, lemon juice, cayenne and mayonnaise.

Fleurons, F. m. pl. (flur'ŏn)—Baked puff paste used for garnish.

Flips—Fancy drink of liquor, sugar, milk, egg (beaten). Example: Sherry Flip. A flip may also be a drink made of beer, cider and spices.

44

Floating Island—Soft custard of milk, eggs, sugar, salt and vanilla is boiled gently and poured into custard cups or sherbet glasses. Beaten egg white, stiffened with powdered sugar, is dropped by the spoonful in a shallow pan containing enough water to cover the bottom. These "islands" are cooked in the oven until firm, then dropped on top of the custard. Chilled before serving.

Flor Alpina*, I. (flōr äl pēē′nä)—Brand of golden yellow Italian cordial.

Florentine, à la, F. (flor ŏn teen′)—With spinach.

Florentine Eggs, F. (oeufs à la Florentine)—Poached eggs on boiled spinach topped with grated cheese and seasoning. Cream added. Baked in a buttered dish.

Florida Gazpachy Salad—Tomatoes, cucumbers, green peppers, onions, hard tack, served ice cold on lettuce. Sour cream dressing.

Flower Jelly—Jellied salad or dessert in which are imbedded edible flowers, such as nasturtiums.

Foamy Orange or Lemon Sauces—Egg yolk beaten until thick with sugar. Juice of orange and lemon added. Grated rind for aroma. Stiffly-beaten egg white (with sugar) folded in just before serving.

Foie, F. m. (fwä)—Liver.

Foie gras, F. m. (fwä grä)—Fatted goose liver usually served as a spreadable paste.

Folding in—Cooking term referring to a method of blending the ingredients, such as folding in beaten egg whites to make a custard light and fluffy. See Chiffon Pie.

Fondant, F. m. (fŏn dän)—Boiled sugar kneaded until it is smooth and creamy. Foundation for many candies (especially French) and filling for dates, figs, etc.

Fonds d'artichauts, F. m. pl. (fŏn′där′tēē sho)—Artichoke hearts.

Fondu, -e, F. (fŏn dū′)—Melted to pouring consistency.

Fondue, D. (fŏn dū′)—Cheese dish. See Welsh rarebit.

Forcemeat—Chopped meats and seasoning used for stuffing.

Fortified Wines—Wines with brandy added.

Frais, F. m., fraiche, F. f. (frai or fraish)—Cool, fresh.

Fraises, F. f. pl. (fraiz)—Strawberries.

Framboises, F. f. pl. (främ bwäs′)—Raspberries.

Française, a la, F. (frän säys′)—In the French manner.

Françoise Sauce, F. (à la frän swäs)—Pink sauce. Example: Béchamel blended with minced onion and tomato puree.

Franconia Potatoes—Raw potatoes pared and baked until brown around a roast.

Française Salad—Chives, Cos lettuce, tarragon, chervil with French dressing.

Frankfurter

Frankfurter—Sausage of pork and beef, highly seasoned and stuffed in casing. More recently, franks may be molded without casing. Varieties added: fishfurters, chicken furters, etc.

Frappé, F. m. (frä pä')—Water ice, beaten and served in tall dessert glasses. May be blended in layers with colorful jellies or syrups. Topped with whipped cream.

French Bread—See Vienna Bread. Without milk.

French Dressing—Salad oil (olive or vegetable), vinegar or lemon juice, salt, pepper, mustard, a dash of sugar to take the "edge" off the vinegar, and a little water added to aid emulsifying.

French Drip Coffee—Boiling water poured over finely-ground coffee and allowed to drip through into the bottom of the container.

French-fried Potatoes, Pommes frites, F. (pom freet)—Raw potatoes pared and cut into lengthwise sections, then fried in deep fat. Their popularity has reached almost epidemic proportions. Result: variations in preparation and service.

French-fried Steak—Small squares of round steak fried in deep hot fat.

French Ice Cream—Rich frozen dessert made with fresh medium cream, egg yolks, sugar and ground vanilla bean.

French Lamb Chops—Made by scraping the fat and meat from the bones of rib chops a little distance from the end. Broiled under a hot temperature.

French Pancakes—Thin pancakes rolled around a filling of currant jelly. Usually branded with a red hot iron. Dessert.

French Toast—Bread dipped into milk-and-egg mixture and fried. Served with syrup or jellies.

Fricandeau de Veau, F. (free'kän dō de võ')—Larded veal roast.

Fricassée, F. f. (free kä sä)—Poultry, veal or lamb cut into pieces, stewed and served with white sauce.

Frijoles, M. (free hol'ees)—Mexican beans cooked with oil, tomatoes, chili sauce and seasoning.

Frisé, F. (free sä')—Curled up, like fried or broiled bacon. Frizzled.

Frit, -e, F. (free or freet)—Fried.

Fritters—Food dipped in batter and fried. Examples: apple fritters, corn fritters, etc.

Fritto Misto, I. (free tō mĭs'tō)—Mixture of fish, frogs' legs, eggplant, brains, calf's sweetbreads, and tomato sauce.

Friture, F. (free'ture)—Butter or other fat used in frying.

Frizzled Beef—Wafer-thin dried beef fried.

Frizzling—Cooking in small amount of fat until crisp.

Frogs' Legs—(Hindquarters only). Considered a delicacy. Legs are skinned, dried well, seasoned with salt, pepper and lemon juice. Dipped into beaten eggs and fine bread crumbs, then fried about three minutes in deep fat. Luncheon or dinner entree. Served with Tartar Sauce.

Froid, -e, F. (frwä, frwäd)—Cold.

Fromage, F. m. (frō mäzh)—Cheese.

Frosted Coffee—Strong hot coffee poured over shaved ice and vanilla ice cream.

Frosted Foods—Also called "frozen foods." Foods frozen by the quick-freezing method developed by Clarence Birdseye. Purpose: Quick-freezing (as in making ice cream) produces fine-grained crystals which congeal without breaking the tissues or outer coating (as in peas or meat). Natural juices are not allowed to ooze out as they would if food were frozen outdoors in winter. Flavor is retained through quick-freezing.

Frosted Grapes—Grape clusters washed and dried, dipped in beaten egg white and, when nearly dry, dusted with confectioner's sugar.

Frosting—Outer coating of sugary concoctions poured over cakes or cup cakes. Examples: Butter-cream, marshmallow, caramel, chocolate, fudge, coconut.

Fruit Fool—Sieved pulp of stewed or fresh fruit mixed with beaten egg whites, sugar and sweet cream. Examples: Orange Fool, Raspberry Fool, Strawberry Fool, etc. Similar to a "whip."

Fruit Salad—Combination of orange and grapefruit sections, cubed or sliced pineapple, sections of fresh pear, peach halves, etc., on a bed of lettuce. Scoop of cottage cheese in center. Garnish. Alternates: fruit may be cut up and mixed. Canned fruits may be substituted for fresh when price and situation demands. Choice of dressings. Whipped Cream Dressing flavored with orange or lemon juice and grated rind is really de luxe. May be used as a luncheon entrée.

Frying—Cooking in fat on top of range at a temperature of 400°F. In deep fat frying, the food is immersed in hot fat, usually in a wire basket which permits handling without damage.

Fudge—Boiled mixture of sugar, cream or milk and chocolate. When the mixture "balls" in cold water, it is beaten until smooth and poured into buttered pans. Cut into squares when cool. Popular candy. Fudge Sauce: same ingredients but cooked only until it reaches a pourable consistency. Served hot over ice cream, custards or puddings.

Fumé, -e, F. (fōō mä')—Smoked.

Galantine, F. f. (gä'län tēēn")—Food stuffed in sausage.

Game—Edible wild animals such as bear, buffalo, deer, hare, opossum, squirrel, rabbit, reindeer and venison.

Game fowl—This term usually applies to edible wild ducks, geese, grouse, partridge, pheasants, pigeons, quail. squab, etc.

Gammelost—Norwegian cheese made from skimmed sour cows' milk. Strong odor.

Garbanzo Beans, S. (gär vän thō)—Spanish national dish. Made with chick peas.

Garbure, F. (gär būr')—Baked stew-soup of stock, bacon, cabbage, smoked sausages, seasonings.

Garde Manger, F. (guard mŏn zhä')—Cold meat department or person in charge of it.

Garnish—To embellish foods but not in a strictly decorative way. Example: adding a sprig of cress or parsley, but not attempting a definite design such as would be used in creating showy dishes for a buffet display.

Garni, F. (gär nēē')—To garnish or adorn.

Garniture, F. f. (gär nee tūr')—French term for items used in garnishing: olives, cress, parsley, tomatoes, maraschino cherries, etc.

Gastric, F. (găs'trēēk)—Cooking term for a mixture of white wine or vinegar, shallots, spices, ground pepper, etc.

Gateau, F. m. (gä"tō')—Cake.

Gaufres, F. f. pl. (gō frē')—Wafers.

Gaufrette Pomme de Terre, F. (go fret pŏm de tĕr')—Potato wafers or chips.

Gazeuses, F. f. pl. (gä zē ōs')—Carbonated water.

Gefilte Fish, H. (gĕ fill te fish)—Stuffed fish, a Jewish favorite featured especially at holiday time. Enjoyed any time. A posh hotel featured lobster. Guests bribed their waitresses to buy gefilte fish for them and tipped heavily.

Gelatin, or gelatine—Colorless, tasteless brittle substance made by boiling bones, hooves and animal tissues. When granulated or powdered, gelatin is used to make jelly-like dishes such as aspics, desserts, molded salads and mousses. Popular because of low caloric value. Can be made showy for banquets, buffets and parties. Because gelatin has no flavor of its own, it makes a compatible ingredient for flavorful food combinations.

Genepi*, F. (zhä nä'pee)—Trade name for sweet absinthe-type liqueur.

Gentilhomme Soup, F. (zhän tee ōm')—Cream soup made with game stock, Velouté base, and puréed lentils.

German Apple Cake—Like Danish Apple Cake served with custard.

German Fried Potatoes—Boiled potatoes cut in round slices and fried in deep fat, or pan fried.

German Salad—Red cabbage, onions, horseradish, shallots, pickles and sliced frankfurters. Dressing seasoned with Rhine wine, oil, pepper and vinegar.

German Toast—Much like French Toast except that the bread is soaked longer. Delicious.

Gherkins—Small cucumbers. Prized for fancy pickles. Range in size from tiny fingerlings to two or three inches in length.

Gibier, F. m. (zhēē'bēē ā)—Game.

Giblets—Liver, heart, gizzard and trimmings from poultry.

Gigot d'Agneau or de Mouton, F. m. (zhee gō'dän"yō'or zhēē gō'de mōō'tŏn")—Leg of Lamb; Leg of Mutton.

Gin—Strong aromatic alcoholic liquor distilled from rye, barley or other grains. Flavored with essential oil extracted from juniper berries, which gives the typical aroma. Clear white. Useful for concocting a large variety of drinks, such as Martini Cocktails Gibson Cocktails and Collins-type tall drinks.

Gin, kinds of: Dry Gin, London Dry, Holland, Sloe Gin. There are variations in smoothness and flavor. Most are white. Seagram makes a premium golden. Sloe Gin is reddish brown and sweet.

Gin Buck—Cooler. Tall drink. Gin, lemon juice, sugar, seltzer.

Gin Cocktails—Martini: gin, vermouth stirred over ice, served with olive. Gibson: same but served with small pickled onion.

Gin Coolers—Known variously as Gin Collins, Gin Fizz, Gin Rickey. Served in tall glasses over ice. Ingredients: gin, lemon juice, sugar, seltzer. Usually garnished with slices of orange and/or lemon and maraschino cherry.

Ginger—Root of a tropical herb plant grown in East Indies, Africa and China. Ginger root may be boiled and candied as a confection. Or it may be roasted and ground for use as a spice in baking. Ginger is also used as a base for ginger ale. Combined with other medicines, it is known as Jamaica Ginger.

Ginger Ale—A commercially available soft drink containing ginger flavoring, sweetening and carbonated water.

Gingerbread—Brown cake flavored with ginger and molasses. Served plain or with whipped cream.

Ginger Snaps—Crisp spiced cooky flavored with ginger and molasses.

Gingko Nut—Small nut used chiefly in Chinese cookery. Potent odor.

Gitana, à la—Gypsy style.

Gjedost, N. (jĕt ōŏt) Sweet brown cheese made of goat's milk

Glace, F. f. (gläss)—Ice cream.

Glacé, -e, F. (glä sā')—Glazed, iced, frosted.

49

Glaçéing

Glaçéing—Cooking with sugar syrup; glazing, icing, freezing, covering with icing or frosting.

Glucose—Crystalline sugar.

Gluten—Nutritious substance found in wheat flour.

Gluten Bread—Bread made from flour rich in gluten; low in starch. It is eaten by diabetics.

Gluten Flour—Wheat flour from which much of the starch has been removed.

Gnocchi, I.—Light dumplings, Italian.

Godiveau, F. (gō dē vō)—Forcemeat balls. (Ground up, as for stuffing).

Golden Buck—Similar to rarebit. Made with American cheese, egg, light beer, etc. Served on toast or crackers.

Gold Cake—Made with egg yolks.

Golden Dawn Cocktail—Benedictine, gin, vermouth, grenadine.

Goober Brittle—Southern confection. Crisp brittle candy made of sugar, salt, and roasted peanuts.

Goose—Large waterfowl (domestic or wild) which makes an unusual menu treat. Somewhat similar to ducks in shape and texture, but much larger. Roast stuffed goose is prized banquet fare; English favorite for the holidays. Stuffing of quartered apples or chopped celery and onion absorbs some of the "gamy" flavor. Roasting time: about three hours.

Gorgonzola Cheese*, I.—Hard, dry, spiced Italian cheese.

Goulash (gōō läsh)—Stewed beef or veal seasoned with paprika. Hungarian specialty.

Gourmand, F. (gōōr mänd)—One who likes and is a judge of good food. Sometimes word is mistakenly taken to mean "one who eats too much."

Gourmet, F. m. (gōōr'mä)—Connoisseur of fine food and drinks. "One who knows."

Graham (bread, crackers, flour, muffins, etc.)—Made of unsifted wholewheat flour which is said to be more nutritious than refined white flour.

Grand Champagne*, F. (grän shăm pain')—French brandy.

Grand Marnier*, F. (grän mär'nyēä)—Brand of fine Cognac flavored with orange peel. Liqueur.

Grand Musigny, F. (grän mōō sēē nyēē')—Choice red Burgundy wine with delicate flavor.

Grapefruit (Pomelo)—Tropical fruit introduced to Florida by Spaniards in 16th Century. Now improved, it's the "Great American Breakfast Fruit" and is used in many other ways. Name derived because it grows in large grape-like clusters.

Types: with and without seeds; white or pink. Large white sweetish seedless grapefruit are grown in Texas, California and Florida.

Uses: Grapefruit halves are a desirable starter for any meal, often used instead of soup. Sections are fine for salads, fruit cups and desserts. Sometimes baked with wine or liqueur as an exotic dessert.

Grapefruit Juice—Popular appetizer, alone or mixed with orange juice. Good ingredient in mixed drinks. Fresh juice is available by the quart, frozen or canned.

Gras, S. (grä)—Fat.

Gratin, au, F. (grä tän')—Sprinkled with bread crumbs and grated cheese and baked until brown.

Grating—Shredding in various degrees of fineness on graters. Used for spices, vegetables, cheese, or the rinds of oranges, lemons or limes.

Graves, F. (gräv)—District in France which produces Bordeaux wines, usually white.

Gravy, gravies—Sauces made with juices from fried or roasted meats, usually thickened with flour. May be served over meat, potatoes, rice, or bread.

Grenadine, F. (grĕn e̱ deen')—Sweet red syrup made of pomegranate juice; used to flavor and color some alcoholic drinks.

Grenouilles, F. f. pl. (gre̱ noo'ēē)—Frogs. Cuisses de Grenouilles means frogs' legs.

Grillé, -e, F. (grēē'ā)—Grilled or broiled.

Grilling—See broiling.

Grits, Hominy—Corn hulled and coarsely ground. Boiled like a cereal; or when cold, fried like mush.

Gruyere*, F. (grū yair')—Specialty cheese made in France or Switzerland. Domestic variety also available. Usually sold in foil-wrapped wedges.

Guava—Edible pear-shaped fruit used chiefly for preserves or jelly.

Guinea fowl, guinea hen—Domestic fowl with rounded body and dark feathers spotted with white. Originally imported from Guinea (West Africa).

Gumbo (Soup)—A soup thickened with unripe okra pods. Contains onions, green peppers, chicken (fowl), rice, tomatoes, parsley, salt, pepper, and salt pork fat. Noted Southern soup.

Haché, -e, F. (hä shā')–Hashed. Minced.

Hachis de Foies de Volaille, F. (hä'shē de fwä de vōl eye)–Chopped poultry livers.

Haddon Hall Salad–Romaine, tomatoes, avocado, chopped walnuts.

Haggis–Scotch dish made of the lungs, heart, etc., of a sheep or calf, mixed with suet, oatmeal, seasoning and boiled in tripe (stomach of the animal used).

Half-and-Half–Half milk and half cream. May also mean half beer and half ale.

Halva–Oriental dessert; paste made with ground nuts, honey and sweet cream. Also a Jewish favorite.

Ham à la Russe–Ham with piquant sauce served in a casserole.

Ham, fresh–Pork steak. Usually roasted.

Ham, smoked–Upper part of a hog's hind leg. Salted, dried and smoked. New processes speed up the "curing" and produce hams which are juicier and tenderer than formerly. Ham is an indispensable staple in many restaurants. It may be served boiled, baked, broiled, fried, diced in cream sauce, or roasted . . . hot or cold. Ground ham makes tasty mousses and croquettes.

Hamburger–Misnomer since it contains no ham. Ground beef, usually seasoned. Probably the most popular single menu item in America. May be fried, broiled or baked. Usually served on a round bun. Sometimes doused with hot sauces (chili) and called "Sloppy Joes;" spread with mustard; covered with melted cheese; or topped with ketchup. A teen's delight is Hamburger and French Fries–all smothered in ketchup. There are Hamburger Heavens and Hamburger Dens and drive-ins of many types which build their business chiefly around the hamburger and boast (like McDonald's) about the millions they've sold.

Hard Ball–Sugar and water syrup boiled at 254°F. until it makes a firm ball when a test portion is dropped into cold water.

Hard Crack–Sugar solution, as above, cooked at 290°F.; remains brittle when dropped into cold water.

Hard Sauce–Butter creamed very soft; confectioners' sugar worked into a smooth consistency. Vanilla, almond, orange or lemon rind grated, or grated cinnamon stick may be added for flavoring. Chill. This is delicious with any hot pudding. Rum optional.

Hard Tack–Unsalted dry hard biscuits. A standard when campers are "roughing it" because of its "keeping quality."

Haricots, F. m. pl. (hä'ree cō)–Beans.

Haricots verts, F. m. pl. (hä′ree cō vair″)—Green string beans.

Harlequin, F. (här lee căn′)—Ice creams of various colors frozen in layers.

Harvard Beets—Boiled beets, skinned and quartered or sliced (unless very small). Combined with a sweet-sour sauce of butter, vinegar, water and sugar thickened slightly with cornstarch. May be flavored with grated orange or orange extract.

Hassenpfeffer, G. (hässen fĕffĕr′)—Rabbit stew. German specialty.

Hashed Brown Potatoes—Boiled potatoes chopped and seasoned with salt and pepper. Packed firmly into heated oil or drippings in a hot frying pan. Cook slowly without stirring until brown. Fold over like an omelet.

Hasty Pudding—Vermont specialty of corn meal, and water cooked in a double boiler one or two hours. Served with maple syrup or sugar and milk. In other regions it may be served with molasses and milk.

Hattenheimer* (hä′tĕn hymer)—German Rhine wine.

Haut Barsac*, F. (ō′bär säk)—White Bordeaux wine.

Haut Sauternes*, F. (o′sō tairn)—Sweet table wines from the Sauterne region of Bordeaux, France. Its California counterpart is a dry wine.

Hawaiian Cocktail—Dry gin, pineapple juice, flavored with both dry and sweet vermouth.

Head Cheese—Jellied, spiced pressed meat from hogs' heads.

Heifer—Young cow that has not yet had a calf.

Hell-Fire Bitters—Wine seasoned with cayenne pepper.

Herb Bouquet—Mixed herbs used for seasoning.

Good chefs follow recipes. Stock pots (shown here) should be half again as tall as they are wide, to prevent rapid evaporation.

Herbs

Herbs—Cultivated plants which are combined with foods to improve flavor. Some plants may be used fresh, like parsley, celery, basil, chervil, etc. "Out of season," most herbs can also be used when dried. Some herbs are prized for their leaves (basil, chervil, tarragon); others for their seeds (caraway, poppy, pepper, etc.); some for their stalks (celery, fennel, etc.); or their roots (ginger); and still others for essential oils used as a base for flavoring extracts (peppermint, wintergreen, dill, etc.). Skill in selecting herbs for specific dishes marks the good cook. Repetition of seasonings in too many foods tends to make all foods taste alike.

Hermits—Cookies made with nuts and raisins.

Hickory Nuts—Nuts of the hickory tree. Edible, but not too plentiful.

Highballs—Long drinks containing liquor and seltzer served over ice in tall glasses. Sweet highballs are made with choice of ginger-ale or other soft drinks to which liquor is added.

Hochheimer*, G. (hōh'hymer)—German Rhine wine.

Hoe Cakes—Griddle cakes of corn meal and milk. Southern.

Hogshead—Barrel holding 63 gallons.

Hollandaise Sauce, F. (hōl än dāz')—Yellow sauce of custard consistency. Egg yolks, lemon juice, butter, salt and pepper, thickened by cooking over boiling water while stirring constantly. Excellent for fish, boiled asparagus or broccoli, Eggs Benedict, and a host of other foods.

Homard, F. m. (hō mär')—Lobster.

Hominy Grits—Bleached hulled corn, coarsely ground.

Honey—Sweet liquid secreted in the nectaries of flowers, gathered and modified by working-bees, condensed by evaporation in cells of the honey comb.

The best extracted honey, rich golden amber-hued, is customarily served at the table for pouring over pancakes, waffles, etc. Darker, less perfect honey is used by bakers, confectioners, cookie-and-biscuit-makers.

Honey is easy to digest. Helps to retain moisture in cakes, cookies, and candies, thereby extends their freshness and edibility.

Flavors vary according to source of blossoms from which nectar is gathered: orange, clover, alfalfa, buckwheat, Scotch heather, tupelo, etc.

Honey Balls—Cross between honeydew and cantaloup melons.

Honeycomb Tripe—Best part of beef stomach. Boiled.

Honeydew Melon—Sweet variety of muskmelon with smooth yellowish rind and greenish flesh.

Hopping John—Southern specialty. South Carolina: cowpeas, rice, bacon, seasoning, all boiled. Alabama: add sliced tomatoes, scallions. Serve with French dressing. Some recipes call for hog jowls instead of bacon. Good luck symbol for New Year's Day.

Hops—Blossoms retard bacterial action in malt beverages, also impart agreeable bitterish taste. Grown: America, Europe and Asia, wild. Cultivated in France, Germany and the United States.

Horseradish—Relish made of grated root of plant of mustard family. Its pungent flavor adds zest to boiled beef, corned beef, hamburger, and many foods. Standard condiment made with vinegar. Fresh, it is prized with seafoods. Combined with dry mustard, sugar, salt, pepper, and heavy cream, it makes a smoother sauce.

Hors d'oeuvres, F. m. (õr dō′vr)—Small appetizers or canapés in a wide variety served with cocktails before a meal. The term now includes many kinds of dips eaten with crackers, potato chips, or thin strips of wholewheat bread or toast.

Hot Rods—Finger sandwiches of deviled ham, dipped in egg and milk and fried as French Toast in butter. Good cocktail snack.

Hotch Potch—Scottish favorite: broth with whole young vegetables.

Hot Cross Buns—Sweet buns made with raisins and decorated with a cross of sugar frosting on top. Lenten specialty.

Huckleberries—Dark-blue variety of blueberries. Smaller than today's jumbo blueberries.

Huile, F. f. (weel)—Oil.

Huitres, F. f. pl. (weetr)—Oysters.

Hungarian Goulash—See Goulash.

Hush Puppies—The hot bread favorite of the South. Made with corn meal, flour, egg, finely minced onion, buttermilk, baking powder, salt and soda. Batter is dipped into hot fat and fried until brown on both sides.

Hydrogenated Fat—Vegetable oil (corn or cottonseed) treated to become solid through the action of hydrogen. This applies to vegetable shortenings used in baking, cooking or deep-fat frying.

Hyssop—Herb of the mint family. Dried flowers and tops are used for seasoning fish, game, stews, sausage and many European specialties.

Ices, also called "water ices" and sherbets—Similar to ice cream except they are made with water and fruit juices instead of cream. Less fattening, hence favored by dieters.

Icing—See frosting.

Indian Pudding—Slow-baked dessert of corn meal, milk, brown sugar, eggs, raisins and seasoning.

Indienne, à l', F. (ä lŏn dee ĕn′)—Dishes originating in India. Sauce: curried Allemande Sauce. Garnish: with curried rice. Curried foods.

Infusion—Liquid obtained from steeping a food, as tea is infused in hot water to extract its flavor.

Iodine—Chemical compound necessary to functioning of the thyroid gland. Without the thyroid, physiologists say, man would be shriveled and imbecile. Sources of nutritional iodine: iodized salt. sea foods (crabs, clams, lobster, mussels, oysters, scallops, etc.).

Irradiated Foods—Treated with ultraviolet rays to produce vitamin D, called the "sunshine vitamin," which is said to have health-improving qualities.

Iron—Compound necessary in foods to enable the body to produce hemoglobin (red blood cells) and body tissues. Lack of iron results in anemia. Source of nutritional iron: eggs, glandular organs (such as liver), meats (lean) and green leafy vegetables.

Irish Moss—Ground seaweed used for thickening.

Irish Stew—Lamb, dumplings, carrots, turnips, potatoes, onions, seasonings. If you want to fancy up your menu, call it by its French name: Mouton or Agneau a l'Irelandaise.

Irish Whiskey—Light gold liquor distilled from barley. Smoky flavor.

Italian Minestrone, I. (mee″nĭs trō′nä)—Vegetable soup with spaghetti and cheese.

Italian Salad—Mixed vegetables (green peas, diced carrots, turnips, string beans) chervil, chives, sliced boiled potatoes, pickled beets. Oil-vinegar dressing.

Italian Salad Dressing—Similar to French Dressing with garlic added.

Italian Sauce—Mushrooms, shallots, butter, parsley, white wine.

Italian Vermouth—Aromatized wine used straight as an appetizer or with liquor as a cocktail ingredient. Sweeter than French Vermouth. Comes in <u>bianco</u> (white) or <u>rosso</u> (reddish).

Italienne, à l', F. (ēē täll′ēē ĕn″)—Italian style. Sauce: Rich, brown; with mushrooms, truffles, tomatoes and herb flavoring. Garnish: with macaroni and artichoke hearts fried in oil.

Jack Rose Cocktail—Apple Brandy, Grenadine, lime juice and sugar. Shake over ice.

Jam—Crushed fruit cooked in sugar syrup to thickish consistency. See Certo.

Jamaica Rum*—Liquor made from molasses in British West Indies. High alcoholic content. Stronger flavor and darker color than Bacardi.

Jambalaya—Louisiana specialty called Jambalaya Lafitte. Made with chopped raw ham, breakfast sausage, minced onion, chopped tomatoes, bacon fat, rice, minced pepper pod, and seasonings. At the end add a dozen fresh oysters and cook only until edges curl.

Jambon, F. m. (zhäm'bōn)—Ham.

Jardinière, F. f. (zhär'dĭn āyre)—Made with assorted diced vegetables and herbs, such as Jardinière Omelette.

Jaune d'oeuf, F. m. (zhŏn dŭff)—Egg yolk.

Jello*—Trade name for prepared gelatin in a large assortment of flavors.

Jerked Beef, also called "Jerky." Long thin strips of air-dried beef.

Jeroboam—Double magnum size, containing 104 oz., as of champagne.

Jerusalem Artichoke—Plant of sunflower family with tuberous edible root which may be boiled or iced for crispness and eaten like celery, raw. See Artichauts.

Jigger—Measuring glass for dispensing liquor. Bar customs vary from 7/8 oz. to 1¼ oz. Large jiggers may hold 1½ to 2 oz.

Jockey Club Sandwich—Open-faced sandwich with imported boneless sardines and melted cheese on toast.

Johannisberger*, G. (yō hänis'bear gêr)—German Rhine wine.

Johnny Cake—Famous Northern bread made with corn meal, eggs, shortening, sugar, sour milk, soda, salt and water. Meal is precooked, mixed with other ingredients and baked.

Julep—Kentucky delight—Long drink of Bourbon, sugar and mint served in frosted glass with ice.

Julienne, F. (zhōō'lēē ĕn")—Potatoes: cut in long slices thinner than for French Fried. Cooked in deep fat until very crisp. Soup: clear soup with vegetables cut in thin strips. Vegetables. Cut in long, thin strips.

Jumbles—Similar to doughnuts but made with sour milk and seasoned with grated nutmeg. Shaped with a doughnut cutter and baked in moderately hot oven.

Juniper Berries

Juniper Berries—Berries of a cedar-like tree. Essential oil pressed from these is used to flavor alcohol in distilling gin. Also used in seasoning venison, soups, stews, and baking.

Junket—Milk, sweetened and thickened with rennet into a jelly-like texture. A mild, delicate dessert.

Jus, F. m. (zhōō)—Refers to natural juices resulting from frying or pan broiling meats, or roasts. Served unthickened, as with roast beef. See au Jus.

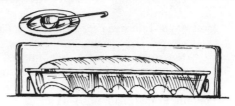

Roasting Pan (Rotissoir), if square or rectangular, can hold oblong meat cuts and fit better in the oven. The board (3 inches to 5 inches high) should be smaller than the pan to permit steam to escape. It holds the meat above the liquid, thus letting dry heat brown the meat nicely. Flavor is enhanced.

Kabob—Pieces of meat (usually lamb or beef) broiled on a skewer. Origin: the Orient.

Kaffee Hag*, G.—Real coffee from which most of the caffeine has been removed. Similar to Sanka*.

Kalak*, R. (kā′lăck)—Highly alkalinized mineral water originally from Russia. Now a proprietary product.

Kale—Non-heading cabbage with loose, curly green leaves. Boiled like spinach. Also called cole or colewort.

Karo*—Brand of corn syrup.

Kartoffel Kloesse, G. (cärt tōffẻl klesse)—Potato croquettes.

Kasha*, R.—Trade name for buckwheat groats. Served boiled or steamed with mushrooms and butter.

Kedgeree—New England dish of flaked cooked fish, rice, butter, minced onion, salt and pepper, curry powder, chopped parsley, and light cream. Thickened slightly with flour. Coarsely chopped hard-cooked eggs added last. Chicken broth optional.

Kentucky Pie—A Southern cream pie with brown sugar, eggs, butter, cream, salt and vanilla. Baked.

Kijafa, D. (kēē yăffä′)—Fortified Danish cherry wine.

King, à la—See à la King.

King size—Extra large, as oversized Martinis.

Kipper—To clean and preserve by salting, drying or smoking fish, herring or salmon.

Kippered Herring—Smoked or dried herring.

Kirschwasser*, G. (kĭrsh′wässer)—Cherry cordial or brandy. Clear.

Kisses—Confection made of stiffly-beaten egg whites, powdered sugar, and flavoring. Similar to "meringues." Baked from 40-60 min. at very low heat. If scooped out and filled with ice cream, they are called "meringues glacées." May also be made with shredded coconut.

Kitchen Bouquet*—Trade name for bottled seasoning used for soups, stews and gravies.

Klim*—Dried powdered milk. Trade name created by spelling "milk" backward.

Kneading—To mix or work dough into a plastic mass by folding it over, pressing and squeezing, usually with the hands. A method of working more flour into the dough. Improves texture. Process used in making breads, raised biscuits, coffee cakes, stollen.

Knishes—Baked pastry canapés, spread with liver-paste or other combination, rolled, cut into small sections and formed into little balls before baking in hot oven.

Knöpfli

Knöpfli, G. (knōff lee)—Small German dumplings.

Kohlrabi—A kind of cabbage with bulbous end resembling a turnip. Cooked like turnips.

Kosher—Food prepared and served according to Jewish dietary laws. "Kosher table" refers to homes or eating establishments, like the internationally-famous Grossinger's, which specialize in providing kosher food.

Koumiss, koumis, or koumyss—Fermented milk of mares or camels. Used for invalids' drink by combining with yeast and sugar. May also be made of cows' milk.

Kuchen, G. (kōō′kĕn)—German coffee cake made of yeast dough covered with sugar and spices. Often contains nuts and raisins.

Kümmel, G. (kimmel)—Cordial flavored with caraway seeds.

La Cote*, F. (lä cōt')—Swiss wines from Lake Geneva or "La Cote d'Or." Region west of Lausanne.

Lachryma Christi, I.—A variety of Italian wines made from grapes grown in crumbled lava on the slopes of Mt. Vesuvius. May be sweet or dry, red or white. Predominantly white and medium.

Lady Baltimore Cake—White layer cake made with egg whites, milk, sugar, shortening, cake flour, baking powder, and vanilla. Layers are put together with fruit and nut filling. Top and sides are covered with a cream frosting.

Ladyfingers—Cookies made of sponge batter and shaped somewhat like a finger. Often used as a base or trim for fancy desserts.

Läger Beer—A beer originally made in Germany, now also in America. It is stored and allowed "to lay" or rest for several months before siphoning and bottling or kegging. Light colored and smooth.

Lait, F. m. (lä)—Milk.

Laitue, F. f. (lä'too)—Lettuce.

Lallah Rookh—Vanilla ice cream with rum flavor.

Lamb—Meat from sheep a few months old.

Langouste, F. f. (län goost')—Crawfish found in salt water.

Langue, F. f. (läng)—Tongue.

Lapin, F. m. (lä'păn)—Rabbit.

Lard—The fat of hogs melted down, clarified and solidified. Used for frying or as shortening.

Larding—Inserting thin strips of salt pork into surface of meat or fish which is to be roasted.

Lardon—Match-like strips of salt pork inserted into dry meat or fish, either into surface incisions or by use of a larding needle.

Lattice Potatoes—Thin slices of raw potatoes cross-cut to resemble lattice-work, then fried in deep fat.

Laurel Leaves—Dried leaves of Sweet Bay. See Bay Leaves.

Lebkuchen, G. (läb koo'kĕn)—Sweet honey cakes. German specialty.

Leeks—Mild form of onion with broad, long succulent leaves. Used as seasoning in soups or stews.

Légumes, F. m. pl. (lä'gūme)—Vegetables, fresh or dried: beans, peas, lentils, etc.

Lentils—Small flat edible seeds of lentil plants (pea family). Used chiefly for soups.

61

Lettuce

Lettuce–Chief salad greens. First used in England when King Henry VIII conferred a special award in 1520 upon the gardener who devised combination of lettuce and cherries for the royal table. Chief types: head lettuce, chiefly Iceberg; bunch lettuce, as Boston, romaine or Cos; leaf lettuces, specialty kinds, as the tender, small-head Bibb.

California grows three crops of Iceberg lettuce a year: late crop in northern part of Central Valley; mid-season crop in the middle areas; and early crop around Salinas. With good refrigeration, lettuce is available all year. Recent improvements in shipping cut costs. California's fruit-and-vegetable-growers' association devised the way to increase contents of crates by cutting off roots and coarse outer leaves before packing on the field. They are left for plowing under. Less cost for shipping. Uses: Crisp fresh lettuce is a prime salad ingredient and garnish. Also used in sandwiches. To retain crispness, lettuce should be refrigerated in humidifier containers or wrapped to prevent it from drying out. Coarse outer leaves may be broken up and served as Dutch or Wilted Lettuce: tossed lightly in a pan containing crisped bacon bits, a little bacon fat, vinegar, water, salt and pepper. Sweet or sour cream is added last.

Liaison, F. (lēē ā′zŏn)–Blending medium, as eggs to thicken soups and sauces.

Lichee Nuts, also spelled Litchi (lēē′chēē)–Edible, sweet, raisin-like fruit grown in China.

Liebfraumilch, G. (lēēb′fräōō mĭlk)–German Rhine wine.

Liederkranz Cheese*, G. (lēē′dĕr kräntz)–Soft, rich, camembert type: spreadable. Trade marked. Strong odor.

Limburger*, G.–Soft, rich cheese with strong odor, originally made in Belgium.

Limes–Small green or greenish yellow citrus fruits similar to lemons, with juicy tart pulp rich in vitamin C. Lend piquant flavor to daiquiris, whiskey sours, punches, or rickeys. May be used for limeade or lime-and-lemonade and for such desserts as gelatins and lime chiffon pie.

Coquille, or shell, can be used for cooking delicious "au gratin" dishes; lobster bits au gratin is one of the many popular shellfish entrees that can be served in shells.

Lingonberry—Berries resembling small cranberries; Scandinavian favorite. Available canned.

Liqueur, F. m. (lēē′kēr″ or lĭ kŭr′)—Comparable to cordials. Strong, sweet, syrupy alcoholic compounds generally served in small glasses as after-dinner topper-offers. Available in many flavors and colors. See Cordials.

Liquor—Distilled alcoholic beverages, such as: bourbon, gin, rum, Scotch, rye whiskey, etc. Includes all whiskies, brandies and cordials or liqueurs.

Lobster—Highly-rated crustacean, deemed to be the most delicious seafood available. Popular in both America and Europe. Eaten fresh along the Atlantic seacoast, where much lobster grows. Canned in immense quantities. Chicken Lobsters, weighing about a pound each, are considered choice and tender. Average weight: from one to two-and-a-half pounds. Large ones, 15 to 20 pounds, are not as tender.

Served boiled, steamed, broiled, baked, creamed in Newburgs or Thermidor. Cold: boiled halves are combined with salad. Lobster salad is supreme on lettuce or as filling for avocado halves or in tomato surprize. Also tasty as a bisque. Lobster claws, combined with other seafood, are served as the famous "Seashore Dinners."

Lobster à la Mornay—Lobster combined with crab or halibut, mushrooms, and yellow cream sauce; served over or with spaghetti.

Lobster à la Newburg—Lobster meat cooked in cream sauce thickened with eggs and flavored with seasonings. Sherry optional.

Lobster à la Thermidor—Cooked lobster meat cubed and combined with mushrooms, butter, Parmesan cheese, and dry mustard. Sherry wine optional, but usual. Poured into lobster shells and browned in moderate oven.

Lobster Créole—Diced lobster meat with sauce containing tomatoes, green pepper, butter and flavored with white wine. Served with or without rice.

Lobster Bisque or Soup—Cream soup with chopped lobster meat. Strained or not.

Lobster, Stuffed—Live lobster split in half lengthwise. Stomach and intestinal canal removed. Large claws cracked. Body-shell stuffed with mixture of roe, bread crumbs, butter, minced onions and seasonings. Baked in moderate oven.

Loganberry—Hybrid of blackberry and red raspberry plants, fruit of. Very tasty for pies, jams, jellies or compotes of stewed fruits.

Loin—Portion of a carcass between the ribs and hind leg, along either side of the spine. Usually very tender.

London Broil

London Broil—Originally a combination of meats: lamb chop, kidney, small sausage, etc. Now, usually a large section of beef flank broiled to the degree preferred (rare, medium, or well-done), sliced diagonally and served with Bordelaise Sauce.

London Dry Gin—Originally gin imported from London, England; less sweet than American gin. Now, the term applies to a type of gin.

Loquats—Small, yellow, edible, plumlike fruit of a small tree of the rose family, native to China and Japan. Makes good preserves. Similar to Kumquats.

Lovage—Celery-like herb for flavoring salads, soups, stews, vegetables, meats, etc. European herb of the carrot family.

Lyonnaise Potatoes—Sautéed with onions.

Lyonnaise Sauce—Brown sauce with minced onions, herbs and white wine.

Lyon Sausage, F. (lēē ŏn′)—Air-dried pork sausage.

Sliced London Broil on platter with mushrooms and baked potato is a menu favorite. Bordelaise Sauce may be served by waiter.

Macaroni (măk e rō′nĭ)—Along with spaghetti and vermicelli, macaroni is a typically popular Italian food, as are all "pastas" or pastes. Originally a Chinese invention.
Macaroni and spaghetti are hollow tubes, whereas noodles are flat ribbons.
Both are made from hard glutenous wheat, semolina, by machinery which kneads the flour with very little water. Powerful presses extrude the product. Pins in the pipe determine holes of desired sizes.
Uses: boiled and served with tomato sauce; chilled and made into salad; baked au gratin or creamed and topped with bread crumbs. Favorite meat-substitute and Lenten dish.

Macaroon—Small cake made of egg white, ground almonds or coconut and sugar, then baked.

Mace—Outer covering of the nutmeg, dried and ground for use as a seasoning. Aromatic spice from India.

Maçédoine, F. (măs e dwän)—Mixture of fruit cup or jellied fruits.

Maçédoine Salad—Artichoke hearts, sliced or diced carrots, string beans, green peas, and asparagus tips, all marinated in French Dressing and served on lettuce.

Macau*, F. (mă cow′)—Red wine from the Maçau region of the Médoc in France.

Madeira, P. (măd ēr′ä)—Strong white or honey-toned wine from the Portuguese Island of Madeira. Sweet, dry or blended.

Madeira Butter Sauce—Made of butter, grated lemon or orange rind and Madeira or Port wine.

Madrilene Soup, F. (mad ree leen′)—Clear consomme which may be served hot or jellied. Tomato juice may be added or not. Garnished with lemon sections.

Maggi*, S. (măggĭ)—Trade name for Swiss seasoning liquid.

Magnum—Two-bottle size; 52 oz.

Mais, F. (mä ēēs)—Green corn. Maize.

Mais en tige, F. (mä ēēs ŏn tēēzh′) Corn on the cob.

Maize, (māz)—Corn. Originally Indian corn. See corn.

Maitre d'Hotel, F. m. (mā′tre dō tĕl″)—Head of the catering or food service department.

Maitre d'Hotel, à la, F. (mā′tre dō tĕl″)—Similar to "specialty of the house" describing a style of preparation. Sauce: usually melted butter seasoned with lemon juice, salt, pepper and minced parsley. Potatoes: Thin slices cooked in butter and milk with Fines Herbes. See Fines Herbes.

Malaga, S. (mă′lä ge̲)–Sweet or semi-sweet fortified wine resembling sherry, from the coastal region of Spain. Dark gold or brown in color. Made from Malaga grapes. Also applies to white Malaga table grapes.

Malted Milk–Powdered preparation of dried milk and malted cereals. Combined with fresh milk and ice cream and stirred in an electric blender until foamy, it makes an excellent drink. Whole raw egg may be added.

Mango–Tropical fruit with yellow-red rind. When ripe, its juicy flesh may be eaten raw. Unripe, it is preserved or pickled. Now grown in southern United States and shipped to northern markets.

Manhattan Clam Chowder–With tomatoes.

Manhattan Cocktail–Whiskey, dry vermouth and orange or Angostura Bitters. Served with a maraschino cherry.

Manzanilla*, S. (măn zä nee yä′)–Very dry sherry wine from Spain.

Maraschino Cherries, I. (mär äs kee′nō)–Italian Cherry Cordial made from a variety of wild cherries. Maraschino Cherries, preserved in syrup flavored with Maraschino Cordial, are popular as garnish for cocktails, frappés, desserts and tall drinks in general. They add "zip" to the appearance of otherwise bland desserts and drinks.

Marasquin, F. (mä′rä skăn)–Orange Cordial from France or Italy.

Marbled–Lean meat streaked with thin lines of fat; an indication that it is tender.

Maréchale, à la, F. (mär ā shäl)–Minced cutlets with vegetables.

Marengo, à la–Sautéed chicken with mushrooms, tomatoes and olive oil. Garnished with olives.

Margarine (mär′je̲ rĭn, or mär je̲ rēēn′)–Refined edible vegetable oil, sometimes combined with meat fat. Churned with cultured skim milk to the consistency of butter. Usually fortified with 9000 U.S.P. units of vitamin A per pound. Used like butter for cooking or as a spread at the table. See corn. Also see Oleomargarine.

Margaux*, F. (mär gō′)–Blended wine from the Margaux area of the Medoc in France. See Chateau Margaux.

Margeurite (mär gar ēēt′)–Saltine cracker covered with a blend of boiled frosting and nuts or coconut, then browned in the oven.

Marinade, F. (mă ree näd′)–Mixture of vinegar, wine, spices, etc. for fish, meats and salads.

Marinate–To allow food to soak or steep in a marinade sauce so that flavoring may be absorbed.

Marjoram (mär′je̲r äm)–Fragrant herb of the mint family. Leaves (fresh or dried) are used for flavoring foods.

Marmalade (mär′mä lād)—Jam-like preserves made by boiling sugar with the pulp and/or thinly-sliced or shredded rind of oranges, limes and other fruits. Peach and apricot marmalades use peeled cut-up fruits.

Marmite, F. (mär meet′)—See Petite Marmite.

Marquise, à la, F. (mär kēēs′)—Sauce: Hollandaise with caviar. Garnish: truffles and asparagus tips.

Marrons, F. m. (mä′rŏn)—Chestnuts.

Marrons Glaçé, F. (mä′rŏn glä sä′)—Candied chestnut meats, a French delicacy.

Marrow (măr′ō)—The pith or fatty tissue growing inside of the hollow bones of an animal. Edible.

Marrow Balls—Dumpling-like addition to soups. Made of bread crumbs, beef marrow, egg white and seasonings. Formed into balls and dropped into boiling soup; cooked until done. Served with the soup instead of croutons.

Marsala*, I. (mär säl′ä)—Pale golden Italian sherry from Sicily. Semi-dry.

Marshmallow (märsh′măl″ō)—Confection made with the root of the mallow plant. Commercially, a soft spongy candy made of sugar, starch and gelatin combined with mallow root and coated with confectioners' sugar. May be served as candy, toasted, or combined with other foods, such as sauces, mousses, cake fillings and frostings, to "dress them up" with a foamy topping or texture. Also used as topping for such baked dishes as mashed sweet potatoes.

Martini Cocktail—Dry Martinis are made with gin and French or dry vermouth and usually a dash of Orange Bitters or Angostura, stirred (never shaken) over ice. Garnish may be a thin sliver of lemon peel, an olive, or (for a Gibson Cocktail) a small pickled pearl onion. The less vermouth, the drier the Martini. See Vodka Martini.

Martini Cocktail, Sweet—Made as above but with sweet Italian vermouth and a sliver of lemon or orange rind. See Perfect Cocktail.

Maryland Spring Chicken—Fryer cut up and each piece generously breaded by dipping alternately in beaten egg yolk and bread crumbs. May be pan-fried or pan-browned and finished in the oven until tender.

Marzipan, or marchpane (mär′ze păn)—Confection made of sugar, ground almonds and egg white. Variously shaped. Sometimes colored.

Masking—To cover completely, as with frosting or a sauce.

Maté (mä tä′)—South American or Paraguayan tea.

Matelote

Matelote, F. f. (măt e̱ lōt′)—Fish stewed with wine, chopped onions and seasonings to taste.

Matzoth, Hebrew (mät′ sōth, also mätzsō)—Thin flat crackers made of unleavened dough. Important for kosher menus, especially during Passover.

Mayonnaise, F. (mā′ŏn nāz″)—Creamy salad dressing of corn or olive oil, egg yolks, lemon juice or vinegar and seasoning, beaten together. Taste may be sharpened by addition of dry mustard and other seasonings. Forms the base for a variety of salad dressings, such as Thousand Island Dressing, etc.; also for Tartar Sauce served with seafood.

Maywine—White wine flavored with woodruff (herb) and slices of pineapple and orange. Festive springtime drink.

Mazola*—Brand name for a liquid corn oil used in cooking or for salad dressings.

Mead—Fermented drink of honey and water, malt, yeast, and spices. Contains alcohol. Formerly a soft drink of sarsaparilla, carbonated water.

Medallion (me̱ dăl′yŏn)—Small round meat fillets.

Médoc*, F. (mä dŏk)—More great red wine is made in the Médoc region of France than anywhere else on earth, according to wine experts. The finest part of the Médoc is known as the Haut-Médoc, the area where many fine chateau-bottled wines come from. Bordeaux, Claret-type.

Melba Ice Cream Dessert—Vanilla ice cream topped with raspberry syrup and whipped cream. May be served with half a peach or pear. See Peach Melba.

Melba Sauce—Combination of raspberries, currant jelly, water, sugar and cornstarch, cooked until smooth but pourable for serving over ice cream.

Melba Toast—Very thin slices of white bread toasted in the oven until brown and crisp. Enjoyed especially by dieters, without butter. Also served for use with cocktail dips.

Menthe, F. (mŏnth)—Mint.

Menthe, Créme de, F. (krā m de̱ mŏnth)—Peppermint-flavored Cordial; white or green. After-dinner drink as is or served over shaved ice. Also delightful over ice cream or fresh cubed pineapple.

Melting—Making fluid by application of heat.

Melting point—The temperature at which a specified solid becomes liquid. For example, butter has a low melting point, beyond which it tends to "break down" and change in flavor.

Menu, F. (mĕn′ū or mä nōō′)—Bill of fare. List of foods served at a particular meal. See "Table d'Hote" and "a la Carte."

Mercurey*, F. (mêr kū rā)—White wine from the Côte Chalonnaise region of Burgundy.

Meringue, F. (mêr ăng')—Egg whites beaten stiff and mixed with sugar. Sometimes used as a topping for pies, puddings, and such desserts as Baked Alaska, and browned in the oven. Also made into shells to hold fruit or other fillings.

Merignac*, F. (měr ĭ nyăk')—Bordeaux wine.

Meringue Chantilly, F. f. (mêr ăng'shän tē yē)—Meringue shells filled with whipped cream; perhaps over crushed fruit or conserves.

Merlan, F. m. (mêr lŏn')—Whiting, a saltwater fish.

Merluche, F. f. (mêr'loosh)—Torsk. Hake; saltwater fish.

Metabolism (mĕt ăb'ol ĭsm)—Process by which food is converted into protoplasm and transformed into nutrients for releasing energy for vital processes and new material, assimilated to repair waste in the human body. It is a continuous process which sustains life, but depends upon adequate nutrition.

Metabolism Test—Usually performed by a laboratory technician to ascertain the rate at which the human body "burns" food and converts it into energy. Good or poor nutrition is greatly affected by the kind and amount of food intake.

Meuniere, à la, F. (mě nē air')—Style of service. Soup: Velouté of fish with croutons. Fish: dipped in flour, sautéed in butter, served with butter sauce and lemon juice, sprinkled with minced parsley.

Meursault*, F. (mêr sō')—Pale golden dry, yet mellow, wine from the Meursault region of Burgundy.

Mexican Salad—Chopped cabbage, peppers, onions, pimientos, seasoned with vinegar and herbs.

Mexicaine, F. (měxĭ kān')—Mexican style. Sauce: seasoned with cooked tomatoes and minced onions. Garnish: with tomatoes, red peppers, and onions. Chili sauce. Chili con carne.

Miel, F. m. (mē ĕl')—Honey.

Mignon Fillets, F. (mēē nyŏn'fĭllé)—Small tender fillets usually from beef tenderloin.

Milanaise, a la, F. (mēē län āyz')—Italian style from Milan. Sauce: pink Allemande with tomato purée. Garnish: spaghetti or macaroni served with tomato sauce and slices of ham or tongue topped with truffles.

Milk chocolate—12 per cent milk solids combined with chocolate and from 35 to 50 per cent sugar. Contrasted with bitter chocolate which is usually for baking.

Milk Punch—Tall drink of brandy, rum or whiskey combined with milk and sweetening.

Minced Chopped fine.

Mince Meat

Mince Meat—Mixture of chopped apples, nuts, raisins, suet and spices (and sometimes meat) used as a filling for pies or tarts. Holiday favorite as around Thanksgiving or Christmas. Rum flavoring optional. Candied citrus peel and cinnamon may be added.

Mincing—Chopping fine, similar to grinding.

Minestrone, I. (mē nē strō′nē)—Italian soup of vegetables with spaghetti and cheese. Available commercially, canned.

Mint Julep—Celebrated drink originated in Kentucky. Bourbon whiskey, fresh mint and sugar served in tall frosted glasses.

Minute Steak—Sirloin steak without the bone. Usually sliced thin for quick cooking. Fried or pan-broiled.

Mirepoix, F. (mēēr e pwä′)—Thickening and flavoring for Puree Soups. Light-colored Mirepoix for light-colored soups; colored Mirepoix (with carrots, etc.) for more highly-colored soups. May be prepared in advance and used as needed. Puréed peas are used as a base.

Mixed Grill—Originally, French lamb chop, lamb kidney, sausage, mushrooms and grilled tomatoes. Now may be simplified to include breakfast sausage and bacon, and hard-cooked eggs.

Mixing—Combining two or more ingredients.

Mocha (mō′kä)—Flavoring of coffee or coffee and chocolate.

Mocha Cream—Dessert made with sugar, egg, cocoa, water and cream. A mild-flavored, smooth-textured frozen pudding.

Mock Turtle Soup—Soup made of veal or calf's head and spiced to resemble real turtle soup.

Moelle, F. f. (mō ĕll′)—Marrow.

Moka*—See Mocha. Also a brand name for Coffee Cordial sometimes used for cream-type sweet cocktails.

Monastine*, **F.** (mŏn äs tēēn′)—French Cordial.

Mongol Soup—Slightly thickened soup containing tomatoes, split peas and julienne vegetables.

Mongolese Soup—Beef extract, cheese, vegetables, spaghetti.

Montrachet*, **F.** (mŏn trä shä′)—Well-balanced white Burgundy; sweet but not cloying, with a suggestion of tangy dryness. Fine quality.

Montilla*, **S.** (mŏn tē′yä)—Sherry from the region of Montilla, near Jerez and Cordoba which are famous for fine sherries.

Mornay Sauce, F. (mōr nä′)—Cream sauce thickened with eggs, flavored with seasonings and grated cheese.

Morue, F. f. (mō rōō′)—Cod, a saltwater fish.

Moscatel*, also muscatel. **S.**—Rich golden fortified wine. Sweet and strong dessert wine, similar to Madeira.

Moselle*, **G.** (mō sĕl′)—Choice table wine from Germany, grown on hillsides along the Moselle River.

Mousse, F. (mo͞os)–Light frozen dessert made of whipped cream, seasoned and flavored. Now the term also applies to a large variety of gelatin salads and cold dishes which combine gelatin with ground meat such as ham, chicken or veal; are molded in fancy shapes for buffet arrays.

Mousseline, F. (mo͞os e lēēn')–Hollandaise Sauce blended with whipped heavy cream. Fine for fruit salads. Cold mayonnaise sometimes substituted for Hollandaise.

Moutarde, F. f. (mo͞o tärd')–Mustard, or a sauce made by blending Hollandaise with French mustard.

Mouton, F. m. (mo͞o'tŏn)–Mutton.

Mozzarella, I. (mō tzär ĕllä')–Soft Italian cheese.

Mulled Wine–Claret or cider boiled with sugar and spices. Served hot.

Muddler–Wooden or plastic rod with flattened end for crushing fruit or leaves (mint) in a glass used for cocktails or tall drinks, such as juleps.

Muenster* Cheese; also called Münster, G. (minster)–Semi-fine German loaf cheese. Also made in America. Small bubbles widely spaced. Delicate flavor. Commercially available sliced, for sandwiches.

Muffins–Quick breads made with eggs and baked in small cup-shaped molds. May be of white flour, corn meal, bran, whole-wheat, etc. Fruit optional. Also made of yeast-raised dough, as English muffins for toasting.

Mulligatawny Soup (mŭll ĭ gä täw'nēē)–Smooth, slightly thickened chicken soup flavored with curry powder, salt and freshly-ground pepper, onion and crushed garlic. Half milk–half cream is added to chicken stock.

Muscallonge (mŭs kä lŏnj)–Fresh water fish of the pike and pickerel family. Found in the Midwest.

Muscatel, S. (mŭs kä tĕl')–Muscatel grapes grown in Spain. Or wine, sweet or semi-sweet, made in Spain along the coast near the port of Malaga.

Mush–Porridge made by boiling corn meal in water or milk. Hot mush served with butter, sugar and perhaps milk or cream is a good breakfast dish. Cold mush, fried, is good with syrup, honey or jellies. May be substituted for a vegetable. Hot mush is also a base for Southern Spoon Bread, which see.

Mushrooms à la Russe, R. (ä lä Ro͞os)–Fresh mushrooms au gratin. Served en casserole.

Mushroom Sauce–Brown Sauce made by combining fat, flour, stock, sliced mushrooms and seasonings.

Musigny*, F. (mū see'nyē)–Said to be one of the finest wines from the famous Chambolle-Musigny region. Blended from the pro-

Must

duct of several vineyards within the boundaries of the village of that name. One of the best Burgundies.

Must—Juice pressed from grapes before it is fermented in making wine.

Mustard—Ground or powdered seeds of the mustard plant. Obtainable as a dry powder or a prepared paste combined with vinegar and used as a condiment.

Mustard Greens—Popular in southern United States as a cooked vegetable (like spinach) or everywhere as an addition (fresh, raw) to salads.

Mysost—Norwegian cheese made from whey. Light brown in color. Also known as Primost.

Unusual greens—like mustard or spinach—add welcome variety to tossed salads. Salad greens should always be crisp when combined for tossing.

Nalisniki, R. (näll ĭss′nēēkēē)—Russian pancakes stuffed with meat.

Napa Valley—Fertile valley in California famous for growing vines of Cabernet Sauvignon, the principal red-wine grapes of Bordeaux. Noted for its fine clarets.

Napery—Table linen or synthetic materials used for tablecloths, doilies, napkins.

Napoleons, F. m. pl. (nä pō lā ŏn)—French pastry with cream or custard filling; may be topped with frosting. Assorted flavors.

Napolitaine, à la, F. (nä pō lē tain′)—Neapolitan style. Sauce: tomato flavored with Marsala wine. Spaghetti: tomato sauce and Parmesan Cheese. Meats: with eggplant and tomatoes au gratin.

Navarin, F. (nä vä răn′)—Mutton stew with carrots and turnips.

Navets, D. m. pl. (nä vä′)—Turnips.

Neapolitan Ice Cream—Brick ice cream in several layers, such as vanilla, strawberry, chocolate, etc. Vari-colored.

Nebbiolo, I.—Good classic table wine from the great grapes of the same name. From the Alpine region of Italy.

Nectarine (nĕk ta reen)—Fruit. Cross between peach and plum. Juicy, with excellent flavor. Sometimes called "the fuzzless peach." Good sliced with sweet cream or eaten "out of hand."

Nesselrode—Mixture of chopped fruits and nuts used in making ice creams and puddings. May also be served as a sauce over desserts.

Newburg Sauce—Sherry-flavored cream sauce thickened with eggs. See Lobster à la Newburg.

New England Baked Beans—Navy beans (small) soaked overnight, parboiled, mixed with dark molasses, brown sugar, mustard, salt pork, and chopped onions. Slow-baked.

New England Boiled Dinner—Corned beef, cabbage sections, onions, whole peppercorns, and salt. Simmered slowly until meat is tender.

New England Clam Chowder—Cream soup made with milk, chopped clams, and diced potatoes. Thickened.

New England Salt Fish Dinner—Creamed boiled cod with salt pork, potatoes and onions.

New Orleans Fizz—Tall drink of gin, cream, egg white, orange flavoring, and seltzer.

Neufchatel, F. (nĕv chä tĕl′)—Smooth, mild, rich cheese, French or American.

New York Ice Cream—Smooth and rich. Yellow color obtained by using many egg yolks.

Niacin

Niacin—Nicotinic Acid, member of vitamin B family. See vitamins.

Nicotinic Acid (also called Niacin)—A member of the vitamin B complex, useful in preventing and treating pellagra (nervous disorders, skin eruptions, digestive disturbance) caused by dietary deficiencies. This vitamin is found in protein foods like lean meat, eggs, whole grain, cereals, etc.

Nierstein, G. (near'stīne)—Famous German wine from grapes grown on hillsides of the Rhine, just above Mainz.

Nip—Six-oz. bottle.

Noir, F. (nwär)—Black. See Beurre Noir, Cafe Noir.

Noisette, F. f. (nwä sĕt')—Small pieces of lamb meat, minus bone and fat, sautéed or broiled.

Noisettes of Beef Tenderloin—Slices of tenderloin, flattened with the broad side of a cleaver, seasoned and fried.

Noix, F. f. (nwä)—Nuts.

Noix de veau, F. (nwä de vō)—Roasted tenderloin of veal. See Fricandeau.

Nonpariel Sauce, F. (nŏn'pär āyee)—Seafood sauce of lobster butter, eggs, lemon juice, butter, salt and pepper.

Noodles—Flat strips of dried dough usually made with eggs, flour, water and rolled very thin. Used in soups, boiled or baked au gratin and served as a vegetable substitute on the menu. Starchy, therefore, a good substitute for potatoes. See spaghetti. Fried noodles are traditional with Chinese dishes such as Chow Mein. An excellent low-cost "meat-extender" when served with foods like Chicken à la King or Chicken Tetrazzini. New shapes: cut-out letters of the alphabet or small round o's.

Norwegian Meat Balls—Ground beef combined with a little suet. Eggs added as a binder. Sherry optional. Pan-browned. Simmered with water to cover. Served in Brown Sauce.

Norwegian Salad Dressing—French Dressing plus raw egg yolk, anchovy paste, chopped olives and a dash of dry mustard. Yolks of hard-cooked eggs add a colorful touch.

Nougat—Confection of sugar paste and nuts.

Nouilles, F. f. pl. (nōō'ēē)—Noodles.

Nutmeat—Kernel of edible nuts.

Nutmeg—Hard aromatic kernel of an East Indian nut; ground or grated as a spice for eggnogs, custards and puddings, consommes, doughnuts and cake mixes.

Nutrients—The elements in food which contribute to good nutrition: protein, calcium, iron and vitamins. See nutrition.

Nutrition—Process of assimilating food for promoting growth and replacing worn or injured tissues. Essential to good health. Policies adopted by the Council on Foods & Nutrition of the American Medical Association and the United States Government agree that for good bodily nutrition a daily menu should include milk and milk products; bread and/or cereals; oranges, grapefruit or tomatoes; green or yellow vegetables; meat, poultry, fish or seafood.

Nuts, Edible—Many kinds of nuts are important in menus for commercial food service. All have high nutritive value (proteins and oil). A large variety of flavors is available, therefore, nuts can be used in many ways.

Most-used in commercial foods are:

Almonds from Spain

Brazil nuts from Brazil

Chestnuts from Italy, Spain, Portugal, etc.

Coconuts from West Indies, Central and South America, the Philippines and South Sea Islands.

Filberts are grown in America, Italy, Spain and Turkey. Also called hazelnuts.

Peanuts, underground variety growing on vines chiefly in our own South. See peanuts for suggestions on uses.

Pecans from Texas, Louisiana, California and other warm-climate states. The jumbo, thin-shelled types can be shelled without breaking the halves, therefore are prized for garnishing salads, cakes and desserts and for confectionery.

Pistachio from Sicily. Usually sold unshelled, but are shelled and salted for mixing with other nuts as appetizers and after-dinner treats.

Walnuts from France, China, Italy and Japan. Also grown extensively in California, where a system of stamping the shell with a brand name was developed to assure uniform quality.

Nuts contain concentrated protein and oil. Pecans contain up to 71% fat.

Nut butter, also called nut margarine, is artificial butter made by churning refined neutralized nut oils (chiefly, coconut oil) and cultured milk to yield a good imitation of butter.

Nut oils

Nut oils are pressed especially from almonds, coconuts, peanuts and walnuts.

Uses for nuts include:
Appetizers: usually mixed and salted
Breads: light or dark, chopped or ground
Candies: whole, chopped or ground
Cakes: mixed with batter, in frosting or decorating the top
Coffee cakes and kuchen
Cookies
Desserts of all kinds
Ice creams: alone or combined with fruits
Ices and sherbets
Meat substitutes, as in nut loaves
Pies
Puddings
Quick breads
Rolls
Salads
Strudels
Toppings for desserts and salads
Vegetarian dishes

Vacuum-packed nuts are said to retain freshness longer.

Frozen nuts do not suffer as to texture or flavor, but do stay fresh indefinitely. At warm temperatures the oil content of the nuts may become rancid, thereby spoiling the flavor.

Oat—Edible grain of a hardy cereal grass.

Oatcake—Thin, flat hard cake made of oatmeal.

Oaten—Made of oats or oatmeal.

Oatmeal—Oats crushed, rolled, flattened or flaked. Boiled oatmeal is a popular hot cereal for breakfast when served with sugar and milk or cream. Cold boiled oatmeal can be fried as a vegetable. Oatmeal bread, muffins and cookies lend menu variety.

O'Brien Potatoes—Raw potatoes pared, diced, washed and dried; then fried in hot fat until brown. Drained, sprinkled with salt, sauteed with minced pimientos and a bit of onion juice.

Oeuf, F. m. (oef) and plural, oeufs (oefs)—Egg, eggs.

Oeufs à la coque, F. (oef ä lä cōk)—Boiled eggs.

Oeufs à la Neige, F. (oef ä lä nāzh)—Beaten egg whites mixed with sugar and dropped into hot water or milk with a spoon to form egg-shaped balls. When done, Oeufs are served atop a soft custard, to resemble Floating Island.

Oeufs brouilles, F. (oef brōō ēē āy)—Scrambled eggs.

Oeufs Farci, F. (oef fär see')—Stuffed eggs.

Oeufs Frits, F. (oef frēē')—Fried eggs.

Oeufs pochés, F. (oef pō shä')—Poached eggs.

Oeufs sur le plat, F. (oef sũr lä plä')—Shirred eggs.

Oie, F. (wa)—Goose.

Oignons, F. m. pl. (ŏn yŏn')—Onions.

Oils, cooking or salad—Liquid fats, mostly vegetable, pressed from corn, cottonseed, safflower, nuts, olives, etc. A basic necessity in cooking or baking. Liquid oils under various trade names are useful for frying, broiling, roasting and baking. Major ingredient in salad dressings. Cottonseed oil treated by hydrogenization becomes a solid and white shortening used in baking as well as other cooking. Corn oil can be converted into margarine (butter-like compound) for table use as well as cooking and baking. See Olive Oil.

Oiseaux, F. m. (wä sō')—Birds. Edible.

Oison, F. (wä sŏn')—Young gosling.

Okra—Tall plant with long green pods which are used in soups and stews. Typical ingredient in gumbo, a Southern specialty.

Old-Fashioned Cocktail—Served over ice in a flat-bottomed stemless glass and made with choice of liquor, bitters, sugar. Garnished with sliver of lemon peel, orange slice, and maraschino cherry. Sometimes a stick of pineapple is added.

Oleomargarine, See Margarine—Butter substitute made of animal fats, usually.

77

Olive Oil

Olive Oil—Light yellow oil pressed from ripe olives. Used extensively in cooking and salad dressings. Much is imported from Italy. Now also made in California. Delicate nutty flavor. Prized in Italian recipes.

Olives—Small oval fruits of the olive tree, which is grown in many warm countries: Israel, Spain, Italy and the Southern Pacific Coast area of the United States. Green olives are packed in brine and bottled or canned either whole with seeds intact or scooped out and filled with pimiento, almonds or pearl (tiny) onions. Ripe olives are available whole or pitted, packed in brine; also packed without brine in tubs. Both come in many sizes. Valuable addition to appetizer assortments. Small green olives are also used to garnish the all-time favorite, Martini Cocktail.

Oloroso, S. (ō″lō rō′sō)—Basis for all sweet sherries; blended to make "cream sherries."

Onion—Plant of the lily family with edible stalks (as fresh and green, called scallions), and bulbous roots. When dried, onions may be mild or sharp in taste and smell depending on variety. Sliced raw: in salads or sandwiches. Minced or chopped: to season soups, stews, fried or boiled foods. Juice: combined with salad dressings. Chopped and dried: Easy-to-use seasoning for foods. Onion salt: finely ground and blended with table salt. Indispensable seasoning almost universally liked.

Oppenheimer*, G.—Wine from the Rheinhesse region of Germany. Soft and rich. Popular in America. Several varieties: Oppenheimer Sacktrager, Oppenheimer Schlossberg, Oppenheimer Goldberg, and Oppenheimer Herrenberg. These names indicate the vineyards or winemakers, as Chateaux designations indicate French producers of prime wines.

Oranges—Fruit produced by tropical evergreen trees. Grown commercially in Israel, Spain and other warm countries. Extensively grown in Florida and California. Many uses. Orange juice: appetizer and mixer for drinks. Prized for its high vitamin C content. Fresh oranges sliced or cubed for fruit cups alone or combined with other fruits. Sections are combined with other fruits in fruit salads, or used for fancy desserts such as orange shortcake. Slices are extensively used to garnish cocktails and tall drinks. Grated rind gives tang to desserts and fancy hotbreads. Essential oil (from rind) forms the base for extracts and flavorings in baking and candy-making.

Candied orange peel or orange slices are delightful confections.

Orange Bitters—Liquor containing bitter herbs and/or roots, combined with orange flavor. Used in flavoring mixed drinks.

Orange Blossom—Cocktail of gin and orange juice.

Orange Juice—Juice squeezed from fresh oranges at point of service; frozen; canned; or processed as dry powder. Also available as pre-squeezed juice which is kept under refrigeration and dispensed by dairy counters in grocery stores. Fresh orange juice is perishable; loses flavor and vitamin C if left exposed to air for long periods. Should be squeezed just before using at mealtimes. Better squeezed in small quantities at frequent intervals rather than in large quantities too far ahead.

Orgeat, F. (ōr zhä′)—Syrup made of barley water flavored with almonds or orange blossoms. Used in mixed drinks.

Oriental Salad—Fruit salad combining tropical fruits such as grapefruit and orange sections, served with appropriate dressing.

Orvieto*, I. (ōr vē ĕtō′)—Town in Italy between Rome and Florence which produces Italy's most famous white wines bearing the same name. Resemble white Graves wines of Bordeaux.

Oscar Sauce*—Trade name for bottled sauce originated by the famous Oscar of the Waldorf.

Ovaltine—Flavored malt-and-milk powder used for milk drinks.

Over-run—Increase in volume produced by whipping air into ice cream.

Oxtail Soup—Made by boiling oxtail joints and adding vegetables and seasonings. May be wine-flavored. Usually slightly thickened with Brown Sauce.

Oxidation—Process which hastens chemical action by combining oxygen from the air with other compounds. Good reason why foods should not be left exposed to air, but should be covered or refrigerated promptly. This process also speeds up the growth of Botulus Bacilli in improperly cooked foods or exposed foods, thus causing what is known as food poisoning. See Botulus Bacilli.

Oysters à l'Ancienne, F. (ä lŏn sēē ĕn′)—Baked on the half shell with seasoning and a thin slice of salt pork on each oyster.

Oysters—Marine mollusks in hinged hard shells which grow in ocean depths up to 30 feet along the continental shelf, especially in coastal waters of the Atlantic Ocean. These bivalves feed by straining ocean water through their shells, thereby absorbing iodine and other valuable minerals abundant in seawater. Sanitary Control Measures supervised by the United States Public Health Service protect the public in much the same way that milk is safeguarded in interstate traffic. Fresh oysters may be bought either opened or in shells. Some hotels and restaurants buy shell oysters for bar and specialty service and opened or "shucked" oysters in 1, 3, and 5 gallon cans for stews, fried, escalloped and other dishes. Strong healthy oysters keep their

79

Oysters, Blue Points

shells closed or shut them quickly when tapped. Opened or
"shucked" oysters should be Solid Pack, free from liquid.
Never keep shell oysters more than five or six days before
serving; then only in a cool damp place ranging from 35° to
40°F., but not iced. Oysters are graded by size. Shell oysters
may be large, medium or small. Shucked oysters come as
"Straights" (entire output, not graded); "Counts" (large and
perfect); "Selects" (still perfect though smaller); and "Stand-
ards" (ordinary run after removing "Counts" and "Selects").
Oysters are a delicacy which may be served in many ways. Raw
oysters on the half shell are arranged in a circle on large plates,
packed in crushed ice, with a dish of cocktail sauce in the center. See Oysters, Blue Points.

Other ways to serve oysters: panned, creamed, broiled,
baked, fried, en brochette, with mushrooms, bisque, stew with
milk and cream, scalloped deviled, canapes (as pigs in blankets),
fried, or baked, chowder, soup, à la King, à la Newburg,
soufflé, cutlets, fricassée, au gratin, roasted, in pie, or in stuffing for turkey or fish. Menu listings feature such provocative
names as: Celestial Oysters, Oysters Casino, Oysters Rocke-
feller, Oysters à la Poulette, Oyster Bundles (like pigs in blankets), etc.

Oysters, Blue Points*—Trade name for oysters from Atlantic Coast
waters. Much in demand for serving raw on the half shell. See
Sauce for Oysters and Seafood.

Oysters, Lynn Haven*—Trade name for oysters larger than Blue
Points, which may similarly be served fresh on the half shell, or
prepared in various ways. See Oysters, also Sauce for Oysters
and Seafood.

Oysters, Marine—Pickled oysters.

Oysters Smoked—Small smoked oysters packed in oil like sardines.
Excellent appetizers served with lemon juice and cream cheese
on crackers or thin slices of brown pumpernickel or rye bread.

Oyster Sauce—Oyster liquor, butter, flour, lemon juice, salt, red pepper and cream.

Oyster Stuffing—Chopped oysters combined with bread crumbs, butter, diced celery, eggs, grated onion, salt, pepper and poultry
seasoning.

*A tangy cocktail sauce pro-
vides a focal point for buffet
service of Oysters on the Half
Shell.*

Paddle—Small flat wooden instrument for working butter or stirring batter.

Pailles au Parmesan, F. (pā'yā ō pär me̲ zän)—Cheese Straws, served with soups or appetizers.

Paillette Sauce, F. (pā'yĕt)—Velouté Sauce with cream and egg yolk added.

Pain, F. m. (păn)—Bread.

Pain grillé, F. m. (păn grēē ā')—Toast.

Pain Mane, F. (păn măn)—Small rŏlls split and toasted, filled with a sweet-sour mixture of banana pulp; garnished with pimientos.

Palm Hearts—Canned delicacy for salads; hearts of young growth on certain kinds of palm trees.

Panachée Harlequin, F. (păn ä shā'har le can)—Mold of several kinds of ice cream or ices in lengthwise layers.

Panade Sauce, F. (pän äd')—White sauce using water instead of milk.

Panama Salad—Pineapple, orange, grapefruit, cherries and cream arranged on crisp lettuce.

Pan Broiling—Cooking in a hot uncovered skillet with very little fat; excess fat poured off.

Pancake—Thin flat cake of batter fried on a griddle or pan. Many kinds: apple, bread crumb, buckwheat, corn meal, flannel cakes, French, jelly, potato, rice, sour milk, sweet milk, etc. See Griddle Cakes.

Pandowdy—Baked dessert of apples like a deep-dish pie with top crust only. Long slow bake.

Pané, F. (pän ā')—Breaded.

Pan Frying—To cook in an open skillet on top of the range, usually with a small amount of fat.

Panned Fish—Dipped in bread crumbs, flour or corn meal, and egg, then fried in deep fat.

Panned Oysters—Laid in shallow dripping pan, covered with small amount of oyster-juice, merely heated through in hot oven and served on buttered toast.

Panocha—Mexican candy of milk, nuts, and brown sugar. Boiled to the soft-ball stage. When lukewarm, beaten until creamy, poured into buttered pan to cool, then cut into squares.

Papaw, also **Pawpaw**—Mild flavored fruit of a tree of the custard-apple family, grown in the southern part of the United States.

Papaya—Yellowish-orange fruit resembling melon. Grows on a palm-like tropical tree found in Hawaii, the Philippines and certain parts of the United States. Eaten raw or cooked. Valued for its juice; used in exotic mixed drinks.

Paprika

Paprika—Mild red condiment ground from dried fruit of the capsicum plant. Adds dash to the appearance of salads and pale, bland foods (like rice and potatoes) without much effect on flavor.

Paprika Schnitzel—Similar to Vienna or Weiner Schnitzel. Seasoned flour pounded into slices of veal. Pan-fried until brown on both sides. Served with wedges of lemon. Sometimes served with cream sauce made by adding sweet cream when done.

Paradise Island Punch—Similar to lemon punch with addition of pineapple juice, oranges, grapefruit, and crushed strawberries. Wine may be added if desired.

Parboiling—To boil until partially cooked, as in preparation for roasting.

Parching—To dry up with heat; usually to brown with dry heat.

Pare, paring—To cut or trim away rind, peel, or skin from fruit or vegetables.

Parfait, F. m. (pär fä)—Dessert made by pouring a hot thick syrup over beaten egg yolks or beaten egg whites, adding whipped cream and packing the mixture for freezing without stirring. Also applied to a mixture of ice cream and colored syrup (chocolate, caramel or fruit) served in a tall tulip-shaped flared glass; topped with whipped cream and a maraschino cherry.

Parfait Amour*, F. (pär fä t'ämoūr′)—Brand of French cordial.

Parker House Rolls—Soft rolls made from yeast dough with milk, sugar and shortening added. When light, roll ¼ in. thick and cut into rounds with biscuit-cutter. Brush with melted fat and crease through the center with the dull edge of a knife. Fold over nearly double. Brush with melted fat, let stand until very light, bake. Originated at the renowned Parker House Hotel in Boston.

Parisienne, à la, F. (pä reē seē ĕn′)—Parisian style. Consommé: poultry base with vegetables and seasoning. Fish: poached, using three different sauces separately. Meats: with Parisienne Potatoes, asparagus tips or stuffed artichoke hearts, truffles and mushrooms. Sauce: Espagnole Sauce with shallots and lemon juice. Salad: potatoes, chopped beef, hard-cooked eggs, lettuce and French or Hollandaise dressing.

Parisienne Potatoes—Small round balls scooped out of raw potatoes and browned.

Parmentier, à la, F. (pär män teē ā′)—Special style. Soup: potato soup. Omelets, salads, and meats: with potato cubes added.

Parmesan Cheese* (pär me̱ zän)—Hard, sharp cheese usually grated for soups, au gratin dishes, spaghetti dishes, etc. Italian origin.

Parmiciano Cheese*, I. (pär mee tzee ănō)—Italian cheese. See Parmesan.

Parsley—Herb used for garnishing and flavoring.

Parsley Butter—Chopped parsley, butter, lemon juice, salt and pepper. Used over fish, potatoes, omelets, etc.

Parsnips—Plant with long, thick, white root used as a vegetable. Somewhat sweet. May be boiled and served with melted butter or cream sauce; fried, or added to soups or casserole dishes.

Parsnip Fritters—Boiled mashed parsnips with fibrous core removed. Add eggs, milk, flour, shortening, salt and stir to form batter. Fry two or three minutes in deep fat.

Partridges—Game birds, wild or domesticated. May be bought in the frozen meat department. Considered choice for parties and banquets.

Pascha—Russian Easter Cake made of potted cheese, nuts, sweet cream, butter, etc.

Passion Fruit—Small oval fruit with purple skin and yellow flesh. California.

Pasteurized Milk—After Pasteur. Heated to 142°-145°F. and held there for 30 minutes to check activity of fermentative bacteria and destroy disease-producing types. This treatment is mandatory by law in many areas. Valuable for preventing "sleeping sickness." Pasteurization may also be used for treating beer to inhibit further fermentation.

Pastry—Dough made of flour blended with shortening and water; used for pies, tarts, shells, etc. Term is also applied to all forms of pies, cakes, etc. Various methods produce different results: crumbly crust, flaky crust, puff paste, etc.

Pastry Flour—Made of soft or Winter wheat.

Patates, F. (pä tät′)—Sweet potatoes.

Pâte, F. f. (pät)—Paste made of meat or liver, used for canapés.

Pâté, F. m. (pä tā′) Pie or pastry.

Pâté-à-choux, F. (pä tā ä shoo′)—Cream puff pastry.

Pâté d'émince, F. (pä tā dā monss)—Mince pie.

Pâté de foie gras, F. (pä tā de fwä′grä)—Goose liver paste. Prized as an appetizer, or hors d'oeuvre.

Pates d'Italie, F. (pä tā dē täl ē ä)—Consommé with various kinds of Italian paste, such as vermicelli, macaroni, spaghetti.

Pâtisserie, F. f. (pä tēē′ser ēē)—French pastry. Pastry shop.

Pâtissier, F. m. (pä tēē′sēē ā)—Pastry cook.

Patty—Pastry shell used for serving creamed foods.

Paupiette, F. f. (pō pēē ĕt′)—Thin slices of braised meat stuffed and rolled.

Pauillac*, F (pä yäk)—Finest and most famous wine-producing commune of Bordeaux. Three of the greatest red wines come from this area: Chateaux Lafite, Latour and Mouton-Rothschild.

Paysanne, à la

Such a region naturally produces other fine though less famous wines known by their origin.

Paysanne, à la, F. (pāy sän′)—Peasant style, country style, or farm style. Example: cabbage, carrots, turnips, potatoes and onions cooked with bacon or meat.

Peach Bowl—Beverage of white wine, sugar and cut up fresh peaches.

Peach Melba—Ice cream on half peach topped with raspberry syrup and whipped cream.

Peaches—Round juicy fruits with orange-yellow flesh growing around single large pits or seeds. Popular in the United States as components in fruit baskets, eaten raw out of hand, peeled and sliced to serve with sugar and cream for desserts, made into pies, tarts, jams and marmalades, and even peach brandy. Tasty colorful salad ingredient either fresh or canned. Pickled, spiced or brandied peaches are enjoyed as a variant with roast ham or poultry. Also popular when blended with ice cream, sold separately or as a layer in bricks.

Peanut Brittle—Hard candy made of sugar syrup boiled until it crackles when a test spoonful is dropped in cold water, then poured over shelled roasted peanuts in a flat buttered pan. When cold, brittle is usually broken into pieces because it is too hard to cut.

Peanut Butter—A paste or spread made from ground roasted peanuts. Two kinds: 1—completely smooth; 2—with chunks included. Used for canapés, sandwiches, cookies, salads, desserts and candies. See Peanuts.

Peanuts—Kernels of underground seed pods grown on a vine of the pea family. Edible when roasted. Shelled peanuts have many uses in food service. Examples: peanut and carrot loaf . . . . and chili sandwiches . . . and cottage cheese loaf . . . and egg and celery salad . . . and balls or brittle . . . and banana sandwiches . . . and onion sandwiches . . . and orange marmalade sandwiches . . . and pickle sandwiches . . . peanut cutlets, peanut-fig-raisin sandwiches, peanut cookies, peanut scrapple, peanut soufflé, baked in bread, sprinkled over salads, or as a topping for ice cream sundaes plain or combined with such syrups as caramel, chocolate or butterscotch. Salted peanuts are standard at the bar and on most snack trays.

Pearled Barley—Polished. Husks removed.

Pears—Tender juicy fruit grown in many parts of the United States, as far north as the state of Washington. May be used fresh, canned, preserved, candied, pickled or spiced. Excellent for fruit salads, fruit cups, or stuffed and baked.

Peas—Round seeds from the pods of a cultivated plant. Used when young and green, grown on site or canned or frozen or dried. Usually fresh peas are boiled and served with butter or cream sauce. May be combined with carrots, mushrooms or small pearl onions. Indispensable menu item. Dried peas, split, make puree-type soup. Great freezing plants are located in Eugene, Ore., because peas grow best at cold temperatures, as far north as Alaska.

Pecan—Olive-shaped nut with smooth thin shell. Kernels easily separated without breaking. Choice addition to assorted salted nuts for appetizers. Used extensively in pies, cakes and candies. Grown in California and the South, hence available fresh seasonally.

Peche, F. f. sg. (pāish)—Peach.

Pectin—Water-soluble compound obtained from certain fruits and used to aid in jellifying jams and jellies made from fruits which are low in pectin. Example: apples make firm jelly, peaches do not. By adding pectin to jams and jellies made of juicy berries, coagulation is hastened and less boiling (hence, loss) is required. See Certo.

Peafowl—Peacock (male) and peahen. Edible game birds. May be obtained from purveyors who specialize in exotic foods.

Peeling—Removing outer skin of fruits or vegetables. Commercial establishments use mechanical devices for this purpose.

Pekoe—Black tea grown in China, picked while leaves are very young and still have white down on them (meaning of pekoe).

Pelure, F. (pā lūre)—Skin or peel of fruit or vegetables.

Pemmican—Concentrated food used by explorers or long-distance mountain-climbers. Two types: 1—dried lean beef ground and pounded into a paste with fat. Preserved and pressed into cakes. 2—dried beef combined with raisins, suet and sugar. Ground and pressed into cakes.

Pepper—Ground condiment made from dried peppercorns (berries of the capsicum family). Usually grown in the tropics, such as the Orient or the Spice Islands. Used in cooking or added at the table. Comes in white, red or black.

Peppercorns—Dried berries of the capsicum plant. See Pepper.

Pepper Mill—Small portable device for grinding peppercorns at the table. Gourmets make a ceremony of this when serving salads.

Peppermint—Herb of the mint family. Fresh sprigs or leaves are indispensable for the famous drink, mint julep. See Juleps. Fresh mint chopped and sprinkled over cubed fresh pineapple is a specialty in many fine restaurants. May be added to fruit

Pepperpot Soup

cups containing fresh pineapple. Mint sauce (chopped fresh mint, vinegar, salt, sugar, water) hot or cold is delightful with roast lamb. Mint jelly is an acceptable alternate when fresh mint is not available. Essential oil from mint forms the basis for extracts used for mint lozenges, after-dinner mints, mint-filled chocolate wafers, or as a refreshing flavor for chocolate drinks.

Pepperpot Soup—Lamb, mutton or tripe, salt pork, vegetables and seasonings.

Peppers—Large variety of sizes, colors and flavors from pods grown on plants of the capsicum family. Most frequently served in foodservice operations are the large green or red fruit with mild flavor and thick fleshy walls. Fresh peppers are sliced or chopped for combination salads or salad dressings. Cooked peppers offer menu variety. Sliced peppers fried in olive oil or shortening may be served as a vegetable, combined with scrambled eggs, made into Western Sandwiches, added to omelets. Fresh red or green chopped peppers may be added to salads and casserole dishes for color as well as flavor. Stuffed peppers (meat combined with rice or bread crumbs) make a low-cost entree for lunch or dinner.

Perche, F. f. (pāirsh)—Perch, fresh water fish.

Perdreau, F. m. (pāir drō)—Partridge.

Perfect Cocktail—Halfway between two favorites: Martini and Manhattan. Choice of gin or whiskey (50%); dry vermouth (25%); sweet vermouth (25%). Stir with ice and serve like Martini but with cherry.

Pernod*, F. (pḗr nō′)—Sweet liqueur of the bitters family, flavored with anise. May be added to drinks in drops, or diluted with water and drunk as a specialty. May be deceptive because it is actually stronger than brandy. Imported from France.

Perrier Water*, F. (pā′ree ā)—Mineral water from France.

Persil, F. m. (pair′scc)—Parsley.

Persilé, F. (pair′sēē ā″)—Garnished or sprinkled with parsley.

Persian Melons—Large round melons with netted yellow skin and pink flesh. California.

Petit, -e, F. (pe tēē′, m.) and (pe tēēt′, f.)—Small.

Petite Marmite, F. (peteet′mär meet″)—Cooked beef cut into small pieces, cooked in vegetable stock with cut up carrots, turnips, leeks, and string beans. Served in small covered pots with slices of toast floated on top. French specialty.

Petit Dejeuner, F. m. (pe tēē′de zhoo nā′)—Breakfast.

Petits Fours, F. pl. (pĕ tēē foor′)—Small cakes completely covered with icing of various colors and decorated. For gala occasions.

Petits Pains, F. pl. (pĕ tēē păn′)–Rolls scooped out and filled with sandwich spread.

Petits Pois, F. pl. (pĕ tēē pwä′)–Small green peas.

Pfeffernusse, G. (fĕffĕr nōōs ä)–Small firm cookie balls popular at holiday-time. Eggs, powdered sugar, flour, grated nutmeg, ground cinnamon, ground cloves, baking powder, assorted citrus peels. Cut with a small round cutter and baked slowly. Dusted with confectioners' sugar.

Philadelphia Cream Cheese*–Brand of foil-wrapped American cream cheese, smooth.

Philadelphia Ice Cream*–Special kind made with sweet cream instead of milk or custard.

Philadelphia Spring Chicken–Rolled in bread crumbs and fried. Served with minced mushrooms, green peppers, etc.

Piccalilli–Relish made of chopped cucumbers, green tomatoes, onions and pickled with spices.

Picayune Fizz–New Orleans favorite of rum, lemon juice, grenadine, egg white, cream. Shaken until foamy. Served in tall glasses.

Picnic Ham–Smoked lower end of pork shoulder.

Piéce de Resistance, F. (pēē ĕs′de rā sĭs täns″)–Main dish of a meal.

Pieds, F. (pēē ā)–Feet, usually pigs' feet.

Pie Plant–Common name for rhubarb. See Rhubarb.

Pies–Baked dish consisting of an under crust, an upper crust, or both. Meat and seafood pies are usually made in deep dishes and are the entreé or main dish. Fruit, custard and chiffon pies are served as desserts. Great American favorite; hence enormous variety of pies is available. Here are a few examples: Two-crust pies: apple, blackberry, blueberry, cherry, cranberry, huckleberry, mince, peach, pineapple, prune, rhubarb, and other fruits or fruit combinations.

Open-face pies: banana cream, butterscotch, chocolate cream, coconut cream, cottage cheese, custard, date cream, lemon, lime, nut and raisin cream, orange cream, pecan, pumpkin, squash, sweet potato, etc.

Meringue-topped pies: chiffon pies, made with whipped gelatin for greater fluffiness. Meringue is customary (beaten egg whites stiffened with powdered or confectioners' sugar and browned in the oven). Marshmallow topping or whipped cream variants are frequently used.

a la mode pies: two-crust pies topped with a scoop of ice cream.

Piesport*, G. (pēēs′pōrt, also called peesporter)–Some of the sweetest white table wine produced along the Moselle River in Germany.

Pigs-in-Blankets

Pigs-in-Blankets—A style of preparing certain foods. Examples: party franks wrapped in pie crust and baked; oysters wrapped in bacon and roasted just until the edges curl; wieners inserted inside potatoes and baked.

Pilaf, Pilaw, Pilau—Spicy Oriental dish of meat mixed with rice. May be poultry, lamb or fish.

Pimiento, or pimento—Red fruit of garden variety pepper, cooked and canned for use in adding color to salads or casserole dishes. Mild flavor.

Pineapple—Juicy edible tropical fruit which may be eaten fresh, canned or cooked. Fresh, it makes delicious desserts when cubed and combined with lemon juice and fresh mint. Excellent in fruit cups. Slices are used to garnish and flavor drinks such as Old-Fashioned Cocktails and Planter's Punch. Canned pineapple slices or cubes are favorite accompaniments to roasted poultry, ham, etc. Crushed canned pineapple is mixed in puddings, made into pies or tarts, etc. It is also added to tutti frutti cake filling. Juice can be served as an appetizer or combined with lemon juice and liquor for cocktails and punchbowl recipes. It can be added to ices, ice creams, sherbets or made into conserves by blending with other fruits (strawberries, rhubarb, etc.).

Pineapple Rum Fizz—Drink of rum, pineapple juice, sugar, seltzer, ice.

Pine Nuts—Small, sweet, thin-shelled nuts from pine cones of some species of pines.

Pink Lady Cocktail—Applejack, Gin, Grenadine, lemon juice and egg white. Shaken over ice until it froths.

Pinot Chardonay, F. (pēē′nō shär′dō nāy)—The fine white grape of Burgundy, now grown successfully in certain parts of California (Napa, Sonoma, Bay, Santa Clara, San Benito and Livermore Valleys). Excellent white wine made commercially by the best of the commercial wineries (Beaulieu, Almaden, Louis Martini and Charles Krug). Prime table wine, also featured at wine tasting parties. French import is also available.

Pinot Noir, F. (pēē′nō nwär)—The great Burgundy grape, grown extensively in California. Also a premium white table wine.

Pintade Rote, F. (păn täd rō tāy)—Roast Guinea fowl.

Pinwheels—Rolled pastry spread with sausage mix, liver paste or deviled ham for appetizers served hot or cold, but better hot. Made with nuts or fruit jams, pinwheels are satisfying dessert snacks. After filling is spread, the pastry is rolled like a cobbler, then cut in quarter-inch slices, laid flat on a cookie sheet and baked until light brown.

Piquant, F. (pēē cän′) or **-e** (pēē cänt′)—Spicy. Highly seasoned.

Piquant Brown Sauce—Seasoned with onions, vinegar, shallots, dill or sour pickles (chopped) and spices.

Pirog à la Tea Room, R. (pēē rōg′)—French pastry type dough, filled with choice of chicken, eggs, chicken livers, mushrooms, etc., and served with a white sauce.

Pirojok, R. (pēē′rō jŏck″)—Puff-cake stuffed with ground meat and well-seasoned. Served with soups.

Pistachio Nuts—Small, pale green kernels of nuts borne on tropical trees. Edible and considered a choice addition to salted nut combinations for service as appetizers. Ground pistachios add piquant flavor to ice cream of delicate green color.

Pizza, I. (pēē′tzä)—Popular Italian specialty made of yeast-raised dough spread with a variety of fillings: tomato sauce and grated cheese; tomato sauce and chopped meat and mushrooms; tomato sauce sprinkled with thin slices of sausage; or any blend the cook's imagination can concoct. Baked and served piping hot as an entree for lunch, dinner, supper or any time customers are hungry. A "filling" dish avoided by weight-watchers. Available frozen as family-size or individual portion pies or in snack-size.

Pizzeria, I. (pēē′tzếr ēē ä)—Big business developed from the popularity of the pizza. Foodservice operation featuring pizzas for table service and take-out.

Plank—Hardwood (oak, etc.) slab used for cooking and serving meat or fish.

Planked Steak—Broiled on a plank under direct heat. Usually garnished with cooked vegetables and decorated with a border of mashed potatoes pressed through a pastry tube. Elegant service for two or four.

Plantain (plăn′ tĭn)—Tropical plant bearing edible fruit resembling bananas. Baked.

Plantation Soup—Southern dish of carrots, celery, onions, soup stock. Milk, butter added. Served with grated cheese.

Planter's Punch—Tall drink of Jamaica Rum (or Puerto Rican or Hawaiian), lemon juice, sugar and seltzer. Served over ice and garnished with fruit slices or wedges, oranges and/or fresh pineapple and maraschino cherry.

Plat, F. m. (plä)—Plate of food.

Plat du Jour, F. (plä du zhōōr′)—Special dish of the day.

Plie, F. f. (plēē)—Plaice, a saltwater fish.

Plombiere, F. (plom bee air)—Candied fruits with ice cream.

Plum—Edible smooth-skinned fruit with a pointed pit. Many varieties. Green-gage plums are usually bought canned and served

Plum-and-Apple Butter

as compote for dessert, added to fruit salads or fruit cups. Purple plums, canned, are popular in pies or tarts; but also good as compote or sauce. Some foodservice operators prefer to bake frozen plums rather than boil them. They claim that shape is retained better, producing a less mushy result, better color with less risk of scorching during cooking. Large reddish plums are choice for adding to fresh fruit assortments, fruit baskets or for serving as fresh fruit.

Plum-and-Apple Butter—Tangy combination to serve as jam for pancakes, French toast, breakfast toast, etc. Plums and apples boiled together and sieved, then cooked with sugar until thick.

Plum Conserve—Pitted plums cooked with skins left on. Lemons added. Boiled with sugar until thick. Used as jam.

Plum preserves—Similar to conserves. This process is generally used for small plums, such as beach or Damson. Distinctive flavor.

Plums, Spiced—Really pickled and spiced. Cooked with syrup made of vinegar, sugar and spices (cloves, allspice, etc.).

Plum Pudding—Rich pudding made with suet, flour, brown sugar, eggs, currants, raisins, nuts, chopped citron peel and mixed spices. May be boiled (as steamed pudding) or baked. Served with hard sauce or choice of liquid sauces. Picturesque as a flambé. Holiday specialty.

Poaching—Cooking eggs, fish, etc. in water that bubbles lightly to prevent overcooking.

Pointes d'Asperges, F. f. pl. (pwän däs pĕrzh′)—Asparagus tips.

Poires, F. f. pl. (pwär)—Pears.

Pois, F. m. pl. (pwä)—Peas. See Petite Pois.

Poireau, F. m. (pwäro)—Leeks.

Poisson, F. m. (pwä sŏn′)—Fish.

Poitrine d'Agneau, F. f. (pwä trēēn dän′yō)—Breast of lamb.

Poivrade, F. (pwa vrad′)—Pepper sauce.

Polenta, I.—Like a stew, containing mushrooms, tomato pulp, onions, garlic, parsley, corn meal, grated cheese and olive oil.

Pollo con arroz, M. (pōyō cōn ärōy′)—Chicken with rice.

Polonaise, a la, F. (pŏ lŏ näz′)—Style of service. Sauce: Velouté, sour cream, horseradish, lemon juice.

Polyunsaturated fats—Found in oils from fish and vegetables. Recommended for low-cholesterol diets. Medical authorities prescribe these for persons inclined to high blood pressure and heart problems. The new soft margarines made from liquid vegetable oils mixed with some hardened products are said to be a good source of polyunsaturated fats. Liquid vegetable oils for cooking and salad dressings are also deemed to be polyunsaturated. See cholesterol, also saturated fats.

Pomegranate—Juicy red pulpy fruit with many small seeds. Rare in commercial food service except when used as a syrup to flavor a dish or beverage, such as Grenadine.*

Pomelo*—Trade name for a kind of grapefruit.

Pommard*, F. (pōm ärd′)—Red wine from Burgundy.

Pommes, F. f. pl. (pōm)—Apples.

Pommes au four, F. (pōm ō fōōr)—Potatoes baked in skins.

Pommes de terre, F. f. pl. (pōm de těr′)—Potatoes. On menus, "de terre" is often omitted.

Pommes Nouvelles, F. (pŏm nū věl)—New potatoes.

Pommes purées, F. (pŏm pū rāy′)—Mashed potatoes.

Pont Neuf Potatoes, F. (pŏn nŭff′)—Cut in long pieces and fried.

Popovers, pl.—Very light, puffy hollow muffins; so-called because they rise over the baking tin. Rare enough to be a great treat. Lightness largely due to eggs.

Pork—Flesh of pigs or hogs. Used fresh, pickled or smoked. Menu staple in non-kosher food service. Great variety of possibilities: barbecued, en casserole, fried, roasted, in pie, scrapple, sausage, as chops, ham, spareribs, etc., pickled pigs' feet or salt pork. Smoked or cured: bacon, loin, hind legs (ham). Ham is so popular with eggs that Americans even order it in Paris! Ham may be boiled, baked, fried, sliced with potatoes au gratin, frizzled for sandwiches, diced in casserole or creamed dishes, a great standby for sandwiches, and ground it makes a tasty spread as deviled ham, or an elegant party mousse.

Porridge—A soft food made of cereal or meal boiled in milk or water until thick. Originally pottage. Good breakfast dish, especially liked by young children.

Port*—Sweet fortified wine. After-dinner drink. Milder than liqueurs, alcoholically speaking.

Porter*—Dark brown bitter beer. Lighter than Stout.

Port du Salut Cheese*, F. (pōr du sä lu)—Semi-hard firm cheese from France or Quebec.

Porterhouse Steak—Cut from the loins. Has the largest portion of tenderloin. Most tender and juicy.

Portion Control—Methods used by commercial food service establishments to obtain even-size portions for all customers: 1—to treat all fairly; 2—to keep control over food costs. Purveyors who process meats for distribution can supply any quantity of portions of a given size of most meats. Chicken growers can ship graded sizes. Idaho trout farms likewise.

Porto*, P. (pōr′tō)—Dark, strongly aromatized wine from Portugal.

Portugaise, à la, F. (pōr tōō gāyz′)—With stuffed tomatoes and tomato sauce.

91

Port Wine Sangaree

Port Wine Sangaree—Port wine, lemon slices, sugar, ice. Often served in a pitcher at table.

Postum—Cereal substitute for coffee.

Potage, F. m. (pō täzh′)—Soup.

Potage à la Reine, F. (rain)—Royal soup. Made of milk, chicken and chicken stock, bread crumbs, hard-cooked eggs and seasonings.

Potage Bonne Femme, F. f. (pō täzh′bŏn fĕm″)—Soup of white beans and vegetables cut in thin strips.

Potage Imperial—Thick cream soup with chicken consommé base. Celery added, if desired.

Pot au Feu, F. (pōt ō fō′)—Meat broth with vegetables.

Potage Marquis, F. (pō täzh′mar kee)—Cream of rice with pieces of chicken.

Pot Likker—Juice produced by boiling turnips, mustard greens or chard with salt pork. Flavorful. Southern.

Pot Marigold—Any plant with edible leaves which may be cooked or used fresh as garnish. Pot herb.

Potato—The white, or Irish, potato, a tuberous root, is the most important vegetable in the diet of America, Germany, Ireland, and many other countries. Most famous U. S. types come from Idaho, Maine, New Jersey, etc. The mealiest potatoes are best for baking. These grow in well-drained, sandy soil.

Good vitamin content, including C, gives potatoes credit for being antiscorbutic. Should not be boiled or baked too long because heat destroys this vitamin.

Commercially served baked, boiled, roasted with meats, scalloped, diced in cream, fried, hash-browned, or cut up in salad. Less frequently used in potato bread and potato pancakes. Or, they may be deep-fat-fried as Saratoga chips, French fries, crisscross, shoestring, etc.

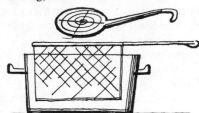

Fry Kettle (Friture) for deep-fat frying should have a high border so that food may be immersed in hot fat. Note fry basket which permits lifting all foods above the fat level. The fry ladle (top) makes it possible to lift only the pieces required for individual servings.

Potpie—Baked meat pie. Deep dish. May have only an uppercrust or be topped with biscuits.

Potpourri or pot-pourri, F. (pō″pōō rē′, or pŏt pōōr′ĩ)—Originally a stew or mixture of highly seasoned meats. Also means a mixture of dried flower petals and spices used to impart pleasant fragrance to linen closets or rooms.

Poultry and game—Poultry includes all domesticated birds that are used for food: chicken, fowl, turkeys, squabs, pigeons, geese and ducks. Game includes wild birds used for food: ducks, geese, partridge, reed birds, quail, plover, pheasant. The flesh of game, except that of partridge and quail, is dark in color and has a fine strong flavor. The flesh of wild birds, except that of wild ducks and geese, contains less fat than the flesh of poultry.

Modern methods of dressing birds cut down markedly on preparation in the kitchen.

Fresh poultry usually has better flavor than that which has been kept in cold storage or frozen; however, modern freezing methods make frozen birds safer to serve than those which have been held a long time after killing and dressing.

Chickens are usually graded by age and size. Broilers are the youngest and smallest. Fryers are a little older and heavier, but still young and tender. Fowl, largest and oldest, may also be tougher. Usually boiled or roasted.

Capons are roosters which were castrated when very young. They grow to 6 or 7 pounds or more and are more tender than roosters.

Rock Cornish Hens, smallest of all, are usually sold frozen. Compact little bodies are meaty and tender and may be stuffed and roasted. Also available ready-stuffed. Average weight about a pound. Raised commercially. Excellent for à la carte and banquet service.

Among the many ways of preparing poultry are: broiled, fried, Maryland (might be called oven-fried), panned, planked, steamed, smothered, roasted, fricasséed, in potpie, pressed, curried, scalloped, creamed, sandwiches, salads, mousses, stuffed, braised.

Poultry, Drawn—Killed. Feathers and entrails removed.

Poultry, Dressed—Killed. Only feathers removed.

Poultry Seasoning—Mixture of spices, herbs and seasonings used to flavor poultry and game.

Pousse Café, F. (poos kä ta)—Rainbow-hued after-dinner drink made by slowly pouring several liqueurs of different colors into a tall slender glass (liqueur-size). Let stand until each finds its own

Prairie Oyster Cocktail

level according to its specific gravity (affected by amount of sugar content). Grenadine (heaviest) tends to settle to the bottom and leaves a cloyingly sweet taste. By mixing brandy with it before pouring, it finds a different level and tastes better. Example: Raspberry, Grenadine, Creme de Menthe, Chartreuse, Brandy, Kimmel, and Crème de Violette. Show-offs serve this as a flaming drink. Check your fire laws; also the durability of your liqueur glasses. Brandy must be on top to get a flame.

Prairie Oyster Cocktail—Egg yolk, ketchup, pepper and a little vinegar. Said to be good for a "hangover."

Praline—Southern candy of pecans, maple sugar and cream.

Prawns—Large shrimp. New Orleans prawns are famous.

Pressure Cooking—Cooking by steam at pressures varying from 5 to 30 pounds resulting in temperatures which may reach up to 250°F. thereby shortening the time necessary to cook food. Care must be used in handling and timing.

Preserves—Sweet concoction of fruit, whole or cut in pieces, and cooked in heavy sugar syrup.

Prickly Pear—Edible fruit of a cactus plant; covered with spines. Exotic rather than popular.

Prime Beef—A-1 top grade. Rare. Excellent.

Prime Ribs—Last ribs of the forequarter.

Primula—Goat's milk cheese from Norway.

Princess Salad—Green string beans, sectioned fresh tomatoes, lettuce.

Printemps Butter—Minted green pea purée blended with butter.

Profiteroles, F. (prō fee těř oles)—Small cream puffs covered with vanilla or chocolate sauce.

Proteins—Chief constituents of plant and animal bodies. Called the body's building blocks. Aids convalescence and helps to maintain good health. Source: cheeses, meats, fish, eggs, soy beans, dried beans, peas, lentils and nuts.

Provençale, à la, F. (prō vän säl')—Provincial style. Sauce: white or brown sauce with tomatoes, onions, garlic, mushrooms. Garnish: fresh tomatoes, mushrooms.

Provincial—Prepared with herbs, gravy, stock and garlic.

Prunelle—Cordial made from plums. Holland.

Prunes—Dried plums. See plums.

Puff Paste—Rich dough for light, fluffy pastries.

Puligny-Montrachet*, F. (pōōl ēē'nyēē Mŏnträ shā')—Superlative white Burgundy wine.

Pulled Bread—Fresh bread with crust removed. Pulled in pieces and browned in the oven.

Pullman Bread—Sandwich loaf, made with milk, baked in covered pans.

94

Pumpernickel—Coarse dark bread made of unsifted rye. Rich in nutrients.

Pumpkin Pie—Open-faced pie made with puréed boiled pumpkin, eggs, milk and seasonings. Could be called pumpkin-custard.

Pumpkin Pie Spices—Blended spices chosen to enhance the palatability of bland pumpkin. Adds variety to cookies, gingerbread, and breakfast buns also.

Punch—Party drink served cold. Fruit juices, sliced fruit, sugar, seltzer and, optionally, wine or liquor. To keep cost down, add cold tea. To sweeten without too much sugar, add gingerale which gives extra zip. Fresh fruit may be floated on top (raspberries, strawberries, loganberries, sliced pineapple). Mint sprigs as garnishes. Kept cold by pouring over ice cubes.

Punch—Aprés-ski drink served hot. Fruits and fruit juices. Use hot water instead of seltzer. Serve in large cups with sturdy handles. Top with cinnamon stick. Garnish with whole cloves.

Purée, F. (poo rā)—Thick soup made with strained pulp of vegetables. This cooking term also applies to any fruit pulp which has been mashed and sieved, such as apples in making apple butter.

Purée de Pommes (de terre), F. (poo rā de pŏm′de tair)—Mashed potatoes.

Pyrex—Fireproof glass in which food may be baked and served at the table without transferring it.

Whipped cream gets the majority vote as topping for spicy pumpkin pie; bits of crystallized ginger add special fillip to whipped cream.

Quail—See Game Birds, also Poultry.

Quenelles, F. (kā nĕl′)—Forcemeat combined with breadcrumbs, egg yolks, butter, salt, minced parsley, lemon juice, and nutmeg. Oysters, optional. Ground into a paste and rubbed through a purée-sieve. Shape into balls, stars, sticks or small squares; dip into egg yolks and brown in the oven. Shapes may be made with a pastry bag and tube. Used to garnish entrées as well as soups. Refreshing change from dumplings.

Quiche Lorraine, F. (kēēsh lō rain)—Deluxe appetizer served at fashionable wine tastings and champagne parties in fine hotels. Made like a large custard pie with a filling of onion-flavored custard with chopped mushrooms and bits of crisp bacon. Kept warm over a Sterno heater. Served in small wedges. Choice addition to an hors d'oeuvres array.

Quince—Golden apple-shaped fruit with hard flesh used primarily for making delicious jelly or preserves. Flavorful enough to serve with meats.

Quinine Aperitifs—As a change from sweet French aperitifs are some Italian aperitifs to which quinine has been added, a bitter ingredient which is strangely appetizing.

Rabbit—Small member of the hare family of edible game. Broiled, fried, in casserole.

Rabbit, Welsh—Dish of melted cheese, well seasoned and served on toast. Eggs optional.

Raccoon—Small tree-climbing animal usually hunted at night. Edible game.

Rack—Market term for the unsplit forequarters of veal or lamb.

Radishes—Salad vegetable of the mustard family. Used as a relish or salad ingredient. Cherry-size radishes are often carved to resemble small roses; used for garnish on salads and picturesque buffet platters of meats (glazed or jellied). Best when young. Tend to get "peppery" when too mature.

Ragout, F. m. (rä gōō)—Thick savory stew.

Ragout of Veal—Cubed left-over veal cooked in brown sauce with seasonings.

Rahat Loukoum—Oriental dessert popularly known as "Turkish Delight."

Raie, F. f. (rä)—Skate, a saltwater fish.

Raifort, F. m. (rä fŏr')—Horseradish.

Rainbow Trout—Game trout native to cold waters of mountain streams and coastal waters of Pacific States. So-called because their coloring resembles rainbows as they flash through the water. Prized delicacy. Also available commercially.

Raisiné, F. (rä″sēē nä')—Grape jam.

Raisins—Dried grapes, available commercially with seeds or seedless. Useful for eating "out of hand," baked in muffins and puddings, combined with other fruits (apples, cherries, etc.) in pies, sauces, and added to nuts in cookies.

Ramekins—Shallow china dishes in which food may be baked and also served.

Ramequins au Frommage, F. m. pl. (rămę kăn ō frō mäzh)—Savory hash topped with bread crumbs and grated cheese, baked in ramekins.

Ramos Fizz—Long drink of gin, lemon and lime juices, sugar, egg white, milk, seltzer and orange-flower water; shaken over ice until it froths.

Rampion Root—European bellflower with thick, fleshy white roots which are used in salads. Herb family.

Rape—Herb of the mustard family. Seeds yield oil. Also a term meaning crushed pulp of grapes after juice has been extracted.

Rasher of Bacon

Rasher of Bacon—Three slices of bacon, broiled or fried. Usually served with eggs for breakfast or lunch.

Rassolnik, R.—Soup made with chicken giblets, veal kidneys, several vegetables, pickled cucumbers, and finished off with sour cream. Russian.

Ravigote, F. (rä vēē gōt′)—Highly seasoned thin white sauce with additional lemon juice, tarragon vinegar, minced shallots, chervil, chives, and melted butter. May be served hot or cold. French mustard optional.

Ravioli, I. (rä vēē ō′lēē)—Italian main dish consisting of small dough casings filled with ground meat, cheese, or vegetables. May be baked or boiled. Served with tomato sauce.

Réchauffé, F. (rä shō fä′)—Reheated. Warmed over.

Red Flannel Hash—New England dish of beets, potatoes, hamburger, seasonings, cream. Browned in a skillet.

Relevé, F. (rĕl wä)—Water ice. Also term for appetizers.

Reine, à la, F. (rain)—Style of preparing. Soup: chicken, chicken stock, milk, etc. Fish: mushrooms, truffles, white wine. Anchovy optional. Garnish: mushrooms, truffles.

Relish—Chopped vegetables well seasoned and pickled. Used for contrast of flavor with bland foods. Many kinds, such as: green tomato relish, hamburger relish (red and highly spiced), chutney, pickles.

Remoulade, F. (rĕ mōō′läd)—Sharp sauce.

Remoulade Salad Dressing—Mayonnaise seasoned with capers, garlic, dry mustard, chopped parsley, and herbs.

Rendering—Melting fat out of suet or other animal fats to free it from connective tissues.

Rennet Powder—Anything used to coagulate fresh milk. Rennin, an enzyme found in lining of calves' stomach. Used in converting milk into junket or cheese. Available also in tablet form.

Revere House Salad—Cream cheese balls, Bar le Duc jelly, served on crisp lettuce with choice of dressings.

Rhubarb—Edible leaf-stalks of a plant formerly called "pic plant." Strawberry rhubarb has redder stalks thereby making more appetizing appearance when cooked. Young stalks are most tender. May be stewed or baked as sauce, frozen as sherbet, scalloped with meringue, made into marmalade or pineapple-rhubard conserve, jellied with apples, blueberries or currants. As its old name implies, rhubarb is tasty in pies (two-crust or custard-type).

Riboflavin—A factor of vitamin B complex found in milk, eggs, liver, kidneys, fruits, leafy vegetables, yeast, etc. Lack of it in diet causes stunted growth, loss of hair, etc. See vitamins.

Rice—Edible seeds of a cereal grass grown in warm climates, such as the Orient or our own southern states. Requires much moisture for growth. Contains starch. Used as potatoes, corn, etc.

Rice, Brown—Rice with hulls on, before polishing.

Rice, à la Créole—Boiled or baked with diced ham, tomatoes, green and red peppers, onions, soup stock. Grated cheese optional.

Rice, Minute—Pre-cooked rice which speeds preparation. Requires only hot water without boiling.

Rice, Polished—Usual form in which rice is bought. Has many uses on the menu: added to soups, curried, baked as pudding, combined with meat in croquettes, or boiled rice borders for creamed dishes, gives lightness to stuffing. See Rice à la Créole.

Rice, Wild—Native rice growing in swampy areas and garnered by hand. Expensive, but considered a gourmet treat with game fowl, especially. Served au naturel, i. e., unpolished.

Riced Potatoes—Boiled and reduced to rice-like consistency by pressing through a ricer.

Ricer—Device for ricing cooked potatoes by forcing them through small holes.

Richelieu, à la, F. (rēē′shĕll eu)—Style of serving. Sauce: Allemande Sauce with tomatoes added. Garnish: mushrooms, artichoke hearts, small potato balls, braised lettuce.

Rickey, gin, rum, etc.—Long drink similar to planter's punch. Made with liquor, fruit juice, seltzer and sugar; served over ice.

Riesling, G. (rēēs lǐng)—The great German grape grown along the Rhine and Moselle Rivers; wine made from. Riesling wine has greater delicacy, floweriness, and natural sweetness. Prime white wine.

Rink tum Tiddy—New England favorite served on toast. Consists of eggs, onions, cheese, tomatoes, butter and seasoning.

Ris d'Agneau, F. (rēē dän yō)—Lamb's sweetbreads.

Risi e Bisi, I. (rēēsēē c̱ bēēsēē) Italian soup containing rice and peas.

Risotto, I. (rēē sō tō)—Rich broth with rice, onions, chicken and cheese.

Ris de Veau, F. (rēē de̱ vō′)—Calf's sweetbreads.

Rissolés, F. (rēē sō lā)—Little turnovers made by rolling puff-paste very thin, cutting into circles, and placing a filling on half of each circle. Edge moistened with water. Other half folded over and pressed. Fillings may be highly seasoned mixtures of ham and chicken or other delicate meat (chopped and moistened with white sauce). Dipped in slightly beaten egg and fried in deep fat.

Riz, F. m. (rēēz)—Rice. See Rice, polished.

Roasting

Roasting—Cooking in the oven with very little moisture. Favorite method for preparing smoked ham, poultry, game, meat loaves, ribroast, leg of lamb, leg of veal, etc. Steamboat roasts of beef may weigh 60 pounds. Roasting makes it possible to provide rare, medium or well-done portions out of the same piece of meat.

Roasting Ears—Corn on the cob, shucked, then wrapped in a layer or two of green husks and roasted in hot coals of an outdoor fire. A favorite at clambakes and barbecues.

Robert Sauce—The French call it "Sauce Rō bear". Brown sauce made with thickened soup stock, lemon juice, minced onions, dry mustard, and white wine.

Rob Roy—Cocktail made with Scotch Whiskey, bitters, and dry Vermouth.

Rock-and-Rye—Rye Whiskey and syrup made by dissolving (or melting) rock candy.

Rocks—Firm-textured cookies containing nuts and raisins.

Roe—Fish eggs when still massed and encased in the ovarian membrane. Considered a delicacy when broiled or fried and served with bacon. See Caviar.

Rognon, F. m. (rō nēē yŏn)—Kidney, as Rognon de Veau, meaning Veal kidneys.

Roly Poly Pudding—Pudding with jam.

Romaine, F. (rō main)—Lettuce with deep green straight leaves and marked flavor. Leaves are long and narrow, suitable for boat-shaped salads.

Romaine Ice Cream—Coffee ice cream with rum added. Flambé?

Roman Punch—Lemon ice with rum flavor added to rum punch.

Roquefort Cheese*, F. (rōk fōr)—Firm crumbly white cheese streaked with greenish mold; made from goats' and/or ewes' milk. Produced in France. Blue cheese (similar) is made in Denmark and the United States.

Rose Apple—Pear-shaped fruit from California whose taste resembles apple flavor.

Rosemary—Herb with pleasant aroma and pungent taste. Widely used in Continental cookery for soups, meats and sauces. Poetically, rosemary is a symbol of remembrance and constancy. Leaves yield essential oil with pleasant fragrance.

Rosettes—Cherry-red radishes sculptured to resemble rosettes. Or clusters of roses pressed through pastry tube in decorating cakes. Also candy roses as a finishing touch in cake decor. May apply to any edible paste which can be formed into rosettes to garnish important foods.

Rotie, F. (rō'tēē)—Roasted.

Rotisserie, F. f. (rō tēē se̱ rēē)–Restaurant which specializes in broiled or barbecued meats.

Rouge, F. (rōōzh)–Red.

Rouget, F. m. sg. (rōō zhā)–Red Mullet, a saltwater fish.

Roulade, F. (rū läd)–Rolled, as meat.

Round Steak–Steak from the upper portion of the hind leg. Hip steak.

Roux, F. (rōō)–Thickening agent for sauces and gravies. May contain no fat, a little fat, or half fat and half liquid. Flour or cornstarch may be used as the thickener. Roux may be light-colored for light sauces; cooked until browned for darker sauces.

Royal Fizz–Tall drink of gin, sugar, lemon juice, egg, seltzer.

Royal Soup–See Potage à la Reine.

Rudesheimer, G. (rue'de̱s hymer")–Said to be the most delicate wine of the Rheingau region of the Rhine River in Germany.

Rue–"Herb of grace." Its leaves are blended with cheese and vegetable cocktails.

Rum (also called ron or rhum)–Potable spirit obtained by distilling fermented mash of sugar-cane or molasses, then aged in wood (usually white oak barrels which are charred on the inside, therefore absorb impurities). Kinds: Jamaica rum, Demerara rum, Barbadoes rum, Martinique rhum, Puerto Rican ron, Haitian rhum, Philippine ron, Hawaiian rum, New England rum, Batavia Arak, and formerly Cuban rum.

Rum Collins–Tom Collins with rum instead of gin. Tall drink made with lemon juice, sugar, seltzer and garnished with lemon or orange slices. Served over ice.

Rum Daisy–Tall drink of Jamaica Rum, grenadine, lemon juice, seltzer, served over ice. Garnished with fruit slices.

Rumsteak, R.–Small steak broiled and served with sweet-sour sauce, an unusual menu offering.

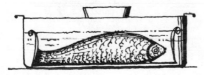

Fish kettle (poissoniere) comes with a bottom grille so that fish can be easily removed without breaking up.

Rusks

Rusks—Hot-bread of quick-rising yeast dough with egg, milk and shortening. Rolled out and cut with biscuit-cutter. Baked at 400°F.

Russe, à la, F. (r$\overline{oo}$s)—Remoulade Sauce with horseradish.

Russian Cream—Sweet dessert of cream, eggs, sugar and gelatine flavored with vanilla, mocha or chocolate.

Russian Dressing—Highly seasoned pinkish salad dressing of mayonnaise, lemon juice, chili sauce, Worcestershire Sauce, chopped pimientoes or chopped green peppers.

Russian Babka—Delicious cake spiced with cinnamon and flavored with rum. Baba au Rhum is similar but soaked in rum prior to serving.

Russian Service—Formal dinner service. Food passed by waiter. Dishes used for each course are removed as the next course is brought in.

Russian Tart—Pastry shell filled with fruit, chocolate or mocha cream. Similar to French pastry.

Russian Tea—China tea served in tall glasses with lemon slices. Some hotels make a ceremony of Russian Tea by serving it in a teapot and teacups with a side dish of lemon slices, whole cloves and maraschino cherries. Cinnamon toast optional.

Rye Bread—See Breads.

Rye Whiskey—Whiskey distilled from fermented rye and other grains.

The tart rates high on dessert lists around the world. In Russia, rich pastry shells are filled with fruit, chocolate or mocha cream fillings.

Sabaillon, F. (sa by on)–See Zabaglione.

Sabayon Sauce, F. (sa by on)–Similar to the Zabaglione dessert but made to a pourable consistency and beaten to a foam. Served with puddings or light cakes. May be flavored with sherry or liqueurs, or orange-and-lemon juices.

Saccharin*–Intensely sweet substance used instead of sugar by diabetics and weight-watchers. No calories. Coal tar product.

Saddle–Market term for the two unsplit hindquarters, as of lamb or veal.

Safflower Oil–Used for cooking or salad dressings, from plants grown in Europe, China, India and Egypt.

Saffron–Orange-yellow seasoning made from the dried stigma of the purple crocus flower. Used to color foods.

Sage–Seasoning made from the dried gray-green leaves of an herb of the mint family. Especially popular for poultry seasonings, soups, stews, and potted meats (beef, lamb, mutton, veal, pork, game). Widely employed in sausage, canned foods, prepared poultry seasonings, or packaged by itself. Aromatic. Should be used sparingly.

Sago–Starch made from the pith of certain palm trees. Used to thicken puddings, cake or pie fillings. Delicate texture.

Saint Emilion*, F. (sän tĕmē yŏn) Bordeaux Claret from St. Emilion located between Graves and Pomerol grape-growing regions of great fame. One of the finest.

Saint Estephe*, F. (säntĕs taif') Claret from St. Estephe in the middle of the famous Haut-Médoc whence come superlative wines known the world over.

Saint Germain, à la; St. Germain, à la, F. (sän zhêr mān)–Style of preparation. Soup: chicken or veal stock with peas and a variety of seasonings. Garnish: green pea purée, carrots and Fondante Potatoes.

Sainte-Hélene Consommé–Julienne of chicken, leeks and barley.

Saki (sakē)–Japanese wine made of rice. Served warm.

Salamander–A broiler-like stove with heat from above and a shelf below. Open front so that dishes may be put on lower shelf for glazing.

Salami, I. (sä lä'mē)–Sausage of pork, beef, and seasonings. Originally Italian. Dried. Usually sliced very thin. Contains garlic usually. May be included in an antipasto assortment (Italian version of hors d'oeuvres).

Saleratus–Baking soda as used in cooking.

Salisbury Steak

Salisbury Steak—Chopped beef mixed with bread crumbs, seasonings, cream or milk. Formed into steak-shaped portions and fried or broiled.

Sally Lunn—Quick bread containing also eggs, milk, butter and sugar.

Salamagundi—Medley of chopped meat, eggs, onions, peppers, anchovies, vinegar and oil.

Salmi—Highly seasoned dish of partly roasted game or fowl stewed in wine.

Salsify—Oyster plant. Its long, fleshy, white roots taste somewhat like oysters. Cooked as a vegetable and served with butter or cream sauce, or used in stews and soups.

Salmon—Game and food fishes of the North Atlantic and the Pacific oceans. Live in saltwater and spawn in fresh. Steaks of fresh salmon are considered a delicacy by seafood lovers. Best broiled, but must not be overdone. Meat is pink when cooked. Canned salmon lends menu variety through many recipes: salads, creamed on toast, baked as a loaf, gelatined as a mousse, etc.

Salt, Table—Seasoning which brings out flavors inherent in foods such as vegetables, salads, meats. Also serves as a preservative (salt brine) for pickling meats and vegetables; and for treating meats to be smoked.

Salt Pork—Pork cured in salt, especially fat portions of hogs' bellies, backs and sides. Used with baked beans, also to yield fat for frying meats and for braising.

Salt-rising breads—Unyeasted breads made of white cornmeal, milk, sugar, salt, shortening and flour.

Samovar, R.—Large kettle for making tea. Usually mounted over canned heat, an alcohol heater, or electric unit to keep liquid hot. Handsome silver samovars lend elegance to formal parties.

Sand Tart—Cooky sprinkled with sugar, powdered cinnamon and chopped almonds.

Sangaree—Hot or cold drink of liquor, water, sugar, with fruit garnish.

Sanka*—Trade name for coffee from which most of the caffeine has been extracted.

Santa Anita Salad—Avocado, tomatoes and strawberries on a bed of crisp lettuce. Choice of dressings.

Sap—Watery juice of a tree or plant. Example: maple syrup and sugar are made by boiling down the sap of sugar-maple trees.

Saratoga Chips—Thin slices of raw potatoes fried in deep fat.

Saratoga Chops—Boned lamb rolled and held together with skewers. Broiled or baked.

Sassella*, I. (sä sĕll′ä)—Italian wine from Lake Como.

Saturated fats–Substances contained in animal products (butter, cream, eggs, milk, fat meats or vegetable oils manufactured as solid substances). See polyunsaturated fats, also cholesterol.

Sauce au Beurre, F. (sōs ō bur̃')–Butter sauce.

Saucisse, Saucisson, F. (sō sēēs', or sō sēē'sŏn)–Sausage.

Sauce Vert, F. (vair)–Green sauce of chives, parsley, chervil, combined with mayonnaise for salads.

Sauerbraten, G. (sour brä'tĕn)–Rump or sirloin beef seasoned with onions and vinegar. Served with thick brown sauce.

Sauerkraut, G.–Pickled shredded cabbage.

Saumon, F. (sō'mŏn)–Salmon.

Sauté, F. (sō tä')–To cook in a small amount of fat. Turn and brown on each side. Less fat used than for frying.

Sauternes, F. pl. (sō tairn)–Light golden wines from Bordeaux or wine-producing portions of the United States. Vary from sweet to dry.

Sautoir, e, F. (sō twär)–Thick flat copper saucepan.

Savories, pl.–Seasoned desserts such as Cheese Straws, Cheese Biscuits, Cheese Cakes, Deviled Shrimp or Lobster, etc.

Savory–Leaves of an aromatic herb of the mint family. Used for seasoning meats, soups, stews.

Sazarac Cocktail–Famous drink of whiskey, bitters, absinthe or Herbsaint, sugar and lemon peel.

Scallions–Young green onion stalks. Served like celery as an appetizer, or cut into rings, or chopped to season salads and cooked foods.

Scalding–To heat to a temperature just below boiling.

Scalloping–Creamed food cooked in a casserole.

Scalloped Potatoes (or escalloped)–Thin slices baked in cream sauce, usually in a casserole.

Scallops, pl.–Tender sweet shellfish which may be broiled, fried, cooked in cream or Newburg sauce.

Schmiercase, G.–Creamed cottage cheese.

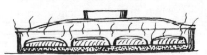

Fish pan (Sautoire) has a low board to make easier the removal of breakable fillets. Tight-fitting cover holds in the steam so that fish may be cooked through, since only part of it is covered with liquid.

Schloss Johannisberg*, G. (shlŏss yō hănnĭs bĕrg)—Famous light golden Rhine wines from the vineyards growing on a castle-topped hill in the Rheingau region. Mild and delicate.

Schnitzel à la Holstein—Breaded veal steak fried and served with fried egg, anchovies and vegetables.

Schnitzel à la Minster—Chopped chicken shaped like a steak, fried and served with sliced oranges and vegetables.

Scones—Scotch quick breads made with butter and milk.

Score—Grade designation for butter. Example: 93-score rates as "extra" or "best." Means butterfat content.

Scoring—To cut gashes as on pie crust or ham before baking.

Scotch Broth—Soup of lamb or mutton with barley, carrots, onions, etc., and lightly thickened. Available canned.

Scotch Whiskey*—Distilled spirits made from malted barley in Scotland. Clear, amber-hued and dry. May be bottled in Scotland or shipped to the United States in bulk and bottled here. Among the most popular liquors.

Scotch Woodcock—Hard-cooked eggs chopped fine and seasoned with anchovy paste or sauce. Served on toast.

Scrambled Beef—Chopped beef mixed with vegetables, hard-cooked eggs, seasonings and sautéed in a frying pan.

Scrapple—Head pudding. Meat from hogs' heads boiled with corn-meal, buckwheat flour and seasonings. When cold, it is sliced and fried. Popular for breakfast or brunch. Pennsylvania Dutch favorite.

Scrod—Young cod.

Scurvy—Disease resulting from lack of vitamin C in the body. Causes weakness, anemia, spongy gums, etc. Used to attack seamen who were deprived of fresh fruits and vegetables while on long sea voyages. See Limes. See also Ascorbic Acid and Vitamins.

Sea Foam Sauce—Fluffy dessert sauce of butter, sugar, and beaten egg whites. Sugar and butter are cooked in water until a thick syrup is formed which "balls" when dropped in cold water. Poured over beaten egg whites and whipped to a foamy consistency. When pourable, it's a sauce. Boiled beyond that it becomes delicious candy, especially when mixed with chopped nuts.

Searing—Browning the surface of meat by intense heat. Example: pot roast meat is seared to seal in the juices before water and vegetables are added.

Sec, F. (sĕk)—Dry, as champagne.

Selle de Mouton, F. (sĕl″de mōō′tŏn)—Saddle of mutton.

Semolina—Meal consisting of hard dry kernels of wheat, used in making macaroni, spaghetti, puddings, etc. By-product of manufacturing refined flour.

106

Semoule, F. f. (smo͞ol)—Fine wheat flour. Cream of wheat.

Sercial (se͂r see ăl)—Dry golden Madeira wine.

Serviette, F. (se͂r′ve͞e yĕt″)—Table napkin, usually cloth.

Sesame Oil—Oil extracted from seeds of the sesame grain grown in East India and China. Blended for salad oil.

Sesamé Seed—Used as topping for cookies, cakes, rolls, crackers and as an ingredient in candy.

Shad—Salt water fish of the herring family which spawns in freshwater rivers. Shad found in the North Atlantic is especially prized as food. Only available around Eastertime. Very full of small bones. Desirable to have the fishmarket "bone" the shad before cooking the filets.

Shallots, F. (Echalotes)—Onion-like plant whose clustered bulbs resemble garlic but are milder. Used for seasoning soups, stews, salads, etc.

Shandy Gaff Long drink made with a split of Bass Ale or beer, a split of imported gingerale or ginger beer.

Shashlik Caucasian—Pickled filet of baby lamb broiled on a spit before an open fire. Served with cooked or raw vegetables. See Shishkebab.

Shashlik of Lamb, R. (Brochette of Lamb)—Lamb seasoned and broiled on a skewer.

Shashlik Moscow—Loin of pork pickled and broiled on a spit. Served with cooked or raw vegetables.

Shellfish—Lobsters, clams, oysters, mussels—any aquatic animal with a shell.

Shepherd's Pie—Lamb or beef (usually leftovers) baked with a topping of mashed potatoes.

Sherbet—Frozen dessert of fruit juice, sugar, water, milk or egg white. Fewer calories than ice cream, but plenty of flavor.

Sherry*—Spanish or American wines, dry, medium or sweet. Pale, golden or amber-hued. Used extensively for imparting delightful flavor to many creamed dishes (Newburgs), drinks (eggnog), desserts. Dry sherries are served as aperitifs before meals; cream sherries are dessert treats because they are sweet.

Sherry Flip—A frothy cocktail with sherry, eggs, sugar and milk.

Sherry Sangaree—Sherry, sugar and lemon slices.

Shirred eggs—Baked in cooking china with butter and cream. Indirect heat keeps albumin (egg white) tender.

Shoe String Potatoes—Cut into very thin strips and French-fried in deep fat. See Alumette.

Shortening—Fat used for making breads, cakes, pies, or pastry. Shortening makes tender dough.

Short'nin' Bread—Southern specialty of butter, brown sugar, flour, etc. Baked.

Shortbread

Shortbread—Scotch origin. Generous amount of butter worked into flour. Cut with cookie-cutter and baked.

Shrimp—Small, slender, long-tailed salt water crustaceans related to crayfish. Source: Atlantic, Pacific and Gulf Coasts. Uses: boiled: in seafood cocktails, salads, Newburgs, casseroles. Fried: dipped in batter and fried in deep fat. Other: Combination platters with a variety of seafoods.

Sicilienne Sauce, F. (sēē sĭ lēē ĕn')—Brown sauce, game stock, fried onions, Marsala wine.

Side Car Cocktail—Cointreau, brandy, lime juice, egg white.

Sidra*, (sēē'drä)—Deep golden sparkling apple-cider from Spain.

Sillabub or Syllabub—Dessert or beverage made of sweetened milk or cream mixed with wine or cider and beaten to a froth.

Silver Fizz—Long drink of egg white, sugar, lemon juice, gin, seltzer. Iced.

Simmering—Slow cooking at just below boiling point.

Simple syrup—Sugar and water in equal proportions boiled until sugar is dissolved. Use as sweetening in alcoholic drinks because sugar dissolves more quickly in water than in alcohol.

Singapore Sling—Cherry brandy, lemon juice, gin, seltzer, served in stemmed cocktail glass.

Sirloin Steak—Choice cut from the hindquarters of beef.

Sirloin Lamb Chop—Chops from the sirloin.

Sizzling Steak—Steak served on a heavy-gauge aluminum platter which has been heated so that steak and juices sizzle.

Skewering—To fasten meat or poultry on long spike during broiling or barbecuing.

Slaw—See Cole Slaw.

Slivovitz*(shlĭv ō wĭtz)—Hungarian Plum Brandy.

Sloe Gin—Sweet English gin flavored with sloes (blue-black plumlike fruits or wild plums.) Reddish brown. Sweeter and heavier than regular gins.

Smash—Drink similar to mint julep. Seltzer on the side.

Smörgasbord, S. (smõr gōs bōrd)—Appetizers or full meals arranged on a large table like a buffet.

Snack—A bit. Small sandwiches or hors d'oeuvres served with drinks.

Soft Ball—238°F. Sugar solution cooked until a bit of it dropped into cold water forms a soft ball. Forms a thread at the third drop.

Soft Crack—Sugar solution boiled to 270°F. at which time a bit of it dropped into cold water forms a hard ball that loses brittleness when taken out of water.

Soirée, F. (swär ēē')—Evening party.

108

Sole, F. f. (sōl)–Flat white European fish. Flounder, a salt water fish, is usually served in the United States.

Solera, S.–Spanish system of blending sherry.

Sommelier, F. (sŏm′ē yea)–Wine waiter.

Sorbet–Sherbet made with a combination of fruits.

Sorrel–Green vegetable, cooked like spinach.

Soubise, à la, F. (soō′bēēs)–Sauce containing chopped or minced onions and melted butter. Named after Marshall Soubise (1715-1787).

Soufflé, F. (soō flā)–Light fluffy baked custard. Cheese soufflé may be served as an entrée. Ditto codfish or other fish soufflés. Dessert soufflés: chocolate, coffee, fruit, lemon, peanut, vanilla. Beaten egg white blended into sauce just before baking produces the fluffiness. Soufflés must be served as soon as they are done or else they tend to "fall."

Soufflé Potatoes–Potato slices fried in deep fat which puff up like little pillows.

Soup–A dish produced by cooking meat, poultry, fish, etc., in water or milk. See Chowder.

Soup-and-fish–Full dress clothes worn on formal occasions. Derived from abundance of food served on such occasions.

Soupcon, F. (soōp sŏn′)–A very slight amount. Literally, a suspicion, as of garlic or onion.

Soupe, F. (soōp)–Soup.

Souper, F. m. (soō pā′)–Supper.

Sour Cream–Dairy-made product useful for salad dressings, cakes, pies, etc. Cream which has been allowed to sour or has been soured by adding a little white vinegar or lemon juice. Can be made with sweet cream, evaporated or irradiated evaporated milk.

Sour Milk–Beverage for invalids. Also useful in baking chocolate cake, doughnuts, biscuits, jumbles, gravies and puddings. In baking, sour milk or cream requires the use of baking soda instead of, or in addition to, baking powder.

Sours–Cocktails made of liquor, lemon juice, sugar and seltzer. Examples: whiskey sour, Scotch sour.

Sous Cloche, F. (soō clōsh)–French style of serving hot entrées. Under bell or bell-shaped or domed cover to retain heat, pending service.

Soused–Pickled, as pickled herring.

Southern Beaten Biscuits–Specialty hot bread of flour, shortening, salt, milk-and-water Mixed. Beaten repeatedly with rolling pin, rolled, shaped with biscuit cutter, and baked. Flaky, light textured consistency because of air beaten in.

109

Southern Fried Chicken

Southern Fried Chicken—Two methods: 1—Dip pieces into cold water, then flour and seasoning. Sauté in a little fat. Drain. Keep hot while gravy is being made. 2—Dip chicken pieces in fritter batter and fry in deep fat until brown. Transfer into casserole and bake in moderate oven 30-60 minutes.

Southern Jugged Soup—Oven-cooked combination of several vegetables with stock from poultry or meat.

Southern Salad—Okra, sweet peppers, etc., mixed with mayonnaise.

Southern Spoon Bread—Corn meal mush with fat and cracklings from pork, beef or chicken added. Well-beaten eggs stirred in. Baked.

Soy Beans—Also soya beans. Edible vegetable valued as a meat substitute. No starch. Little sugar. High in protein. Available commercially as a paste in cheese form. May be cooked similarly to meat-loaf. Soya oil is a valuable vegetable oil used variously in food preparation.

Soy Sauce—Condiment used with Chinese foods. Made from soy beans, salt, etc. Dark brown.

Spam*—Trade name for a canned spiced ham.

Spanish Cream—Molded dessert made with egg yolks, sugar, milk, gelatin and flavoring. Served with whipped cream.

Spanish Omelette—With onions, peppers, tomatoes, parsley, mushrooms, celery and seasonings.

Spanish Rice—With same ingredients as Spanish Omelette.

Spanish Sauce—Minced lean raw ham, chopped celery, carrots, onion, etc. Thickened with flour and fat cooked into a roux and reduced with soup stock and tomato juice to desired consistency. Seasoned with salt and pepper.

Spare Ribs, or spareribs—Pork ribs from which the loin has been removed. May be roasted, stuffed, or barbecued. Often served with sauerkraut.

Sparkling Burgundy*—Bright ruby-red sparkling wine. French. Tart. Resembles champagne in taste.

Spätzle, G. (spätz le)—Little dumpling-like garnishes for stews or soups. Made of flour, baking powder, fat, milk, eggs and seasoned with salt.

Spices—Vegetable flavorings for food. Usually dried, as bay leaves, cloves, nutmeg, cinnamon. Often ground to a fine powder, as allspice, peppercorns, cloves, mustard, cinnamon, curry powder, and the whole range of spices. Gourmets make a specialty of seasoning foods with appropriate spices.

Spider—Frying pan.

Spiral Peel—Starting at one end of fruit (orange, apple, etc.) and cutting a strip of the skin about 3/8 in. wide around the fruit until the bottom has been reached. May be used to garnish a punch bowl.

Spit—Pointed rod to hold meat or poultry for roasting in front of a fire, or barbecuing.

Split—6-ounce bottle of wine, seltzer or beer.

Sponge Cake—Light, fluffy yellow cake made by using only egg yolks (no whites) for leavening. Flavored with lemon or orange.

Spoon Bread—See Southern Spoon Bread.

Sprat—Small herring. Smoked and packed in oil.

Springerle—German cookies, embossed, and usually eaten at Christmastime.

Spritz—A type of cookie decorated with designs in colored frostings. Also refers to a small amount, as "use just a spritz" of this or that flavoring.

Spumoni, I. (spoo mō′nee)—Fancy Italian ice cream.

Squab—Young pigeon.

Spun Sugar—Boiled sugar syrup drawn into fine threads to resemble a fluff of colored wool or cotton. Popular with kids at the circus. May also be used to decorate party table set-ups.

Squab Chicken—Baked in casserole with mushrooms and sliced Virginia ham. Usually refers to a young tender chicken.

Squash, Acorn—Small hard-shelled squash about the size of a large grapefruit. Dark green or green-and-orange shell and yellow-orange flesh. Resembles Hubbard Squash enough to be called mini-Hubbards. Usually cut in half and baked with butter and brown-sugar coating. Each half makes a portion.

Squash Chiffon Pie—Similar to pumpkin pie, but with squash pulp. Gelatin and stiffly-beaten egg whites give the filling its light delicate texture.

Stale Bread—Useful in making bread crumbs for coating croquettes, chops or pieces of meat or poultry for frying or baking. Base for bread puddings. Broken-up pieces are good for stuffings.

Starter-yeast (also called "liquid" or "railroad" yeast)—Potato water, sugar and salt, in which yeast plants are in an active condition. The starter must be stored in a cool temperature to retard yeast action between bakings.

Steaming—Cooking in steam, as in a steam-jacketed kettle or pressure cooker.

Steeping—To soak in a liquid below boiling point to extract flavor or color or both. Example: tea is allowed to steep about five minutes before pouring.

Steer—A young male beef animal which has been castrated.

Steinberger*, G.—Wine from the greatest single vineyard in Germany. Light wine from the Rheingau area.

111

Sterilizing

Sterilizing—Destroying bacteria and micro-organisms by boiling, dry heat or steam.

Stewing—Cooking in a small amount of water on top of the range. Stews usually contain meat and vegetables with an assortment of seasonings. The tougher cuts of meat are suitable for stewing because the slow cooking in liquid improves texture.

Stilton Cheese—English semi-hard white cheese, streaked with blue. Spicy.

Stinger Cocktail—Frappé combining white Créme de Menthe and brandy.

Stirring—Mixing food with a circular motion to insure perfect blending of ingredients; also to prevent sticking to the bottom of the pan or scorching.

Stock—The liquid in which meat, poultry, fish, or vegetables have been boiled.

Stollen, G. (stōlen)—German pastry consisting of yeast-raised dough with eggs, sugar and butter added. It is rolled around a filling of nuts, raisins, butter, sugar and sometimes rum flavoring.

Stout—Malt beverage, dark colored, with strong hop flavor.

Strawberry Chantilly—Dessert of sliced ripe strawberries, egg whites (stiffly beaten), whipped cream and sugar. Desired flavorings may be added.

Strega*, I. (strā'gä)—Golden yellow liqueur from Italy. Sweet and perfumed.

Strudel, G. (strōo'del)—Pastry of flaky dough rolled around a filling of fruit, cheese custard or nuts. Apple strudel is perhaps the most famous. Baked.

Sturgeon—Any of several kinds of large food fishes. Valuable also as a source of caviar.

Sturgeon à la Russe (rōōs)—Steamed sturgeon with a sauce of mushrooms, carrots, onions, tomatoes and garnished with green olives.

Sturgeon, smoked—Usually sliced and used for party platters as lox (smoked salmon) is served.

Sub Gum, or Sub Gam—Base of many Chinese dishes. Bamboo shoots, water chestnuts, mushrooms.

Submarine Sandwich—Jumbo sandwich made by slicing a long ovaloid loaf of French or Italian bread in half lengthwise. Filling: an assortment of meats and vegetables, such as lettuce, cucumbers, tomatoes, ham, cheese, salami, and what have you. Dressing to taste. For serving, slices are cut across; usually thickish he-man chunks. Individual submarines may be made by cutting oblong hard rolls in half and proceeding as above.

Succotash—Corn, lima beans, boiled and seasoned with milk or cream, butter, salt and pepper.

Suet (soo′ĕt)—Fat from meat animals other than pork. Usually harder than pork fat, which is used to make lard.

Suet Pudding—Steamed rather than baked. Finely chopped suet is used as a shortening. Flour, molasses, raisins, sour milk, baking soda, salt, cinnamon, cloves and grated nutmeg. Steamed in covered molds (such as baking powder cans) for three hours. Served with hard sauce or any desired liquid sauce.

Suisse, à la, F. (swēēs)—Swiss style.

Suki Yaki, J. (soo″kē yä′kē)—Japanese specialty consisting of vegetables and choice of meat (beef, chicken, etc.) cooked at the table in front of the guest. The Japanese say it "skee yaki."

Sundae—Ice cream with fruit or syrup poured over. Usually decorated with whipped cream and chopped nuts and topped with a maraschino cherry or fresh fruit.

Supréme, F. (soo praim)—Sauce: made with roux of fat and flour cooked until brown, then thinned with chicken stock. Seasoned with lemon juice and chopped parsley.

Supréme de fruits, F. (soo praim de froo ēe)—Mixture of chopped or diced fruit in cordial. Decorated with Chantilly Cream or Blanc Mange.

Supreme of Chicken—Baked chicken with mushrooms, cream sauce, seasonings and Madeira wine.

Surprise Potatoes—Baked potatoes served in skins (usually covered with aluminum foil). Filling combined with salt, butter and Fines Herbes.

Surprise Tomato—Fresh tomato scooped out and filled with chicken or tuna salad, or any other combination of cold meat and chopped vegetables mixed with salad dressing. May be topped with cottage cheese. Optional. Garnished with a sprig of watercress or parsley. Good luncheon entrée in hot weather.

Suzette Potatoes—Baked in half-shell. Topped with bread crumbs and a whole egg added at the finish.

Swedish Punch—Sweet liqueur.

Swedish Salad—Boiled potatoes, beets, carrots, apples, herring, tongue, pepper and parsley. Similar to a Chef's Salad.

Sweet Basil—See Basil. Herb used for seasoning soups and salads.

Sweetbreads—Pancreas or thymus glands of calves. Usually bought in pairs. Choice tender delicacy. May be broiled, creamed, sautéed in wine, etc.

Sweet Chocolate—Contains from 40% to 65% sugar.

Sweet Potato Pie

Sweet Potato Pie—Southern. Similar to pumpkin pie.

Sweet Potato Pone—Southern. Similar to Corn Pone, with mashed sweet potatoes or yams added. Seasoned with ginger and orange rind (grated).

Swiss Chard—See Chard. Leafy green vegetable, usually boiled.

Swiss Eggs—Baked with cheese, butter, cream and seasoning. Similar to Shirred Eggs.

Swiss Steak—Slices of top or bottom round or chuck into which flour and seasonings are pounded with a special mallet which tenderizes the meat. Browned in fat in a skillet. Water added and the whole is simmered slowly on top of the range or cooked in a casserole in the oven. Flour which has been pounded into the meat produces a tasty gravy as the meat cooks. Should be stirred occasionally to prevent sticking. Gravy may be served over mashed potatoes, noodles, boiled rice, etc. Good way to make the meat dollar go farther.

Switzerland Cheese—Swiss cheese imported from Switzerland. Square or rectangular loaf. Firm texture. Large holes. Favorite in combination with ham for sandwiches.

Swizzle Stick—A stick with a forked end used for spearing or holding the maraschino cherry in mixed drinks.

Swordfish—Large marine food fish with the upper snout extending in a long sword-like point. Flesh is white and close-grained. Enjoyed by seafood fanciers.

Syllabub—Famous English dessert. Stiffly-beaten cream with sugar and a little rum folded in. Served in sherbet glasses after "ripening" in the refrigerator for half an hour (covered, of course).

A tie-in with the decor theme makes the swizzle stick a good merchandiser since patrons often take it home as a reminder of a gala occasion.

Tabasco*–Brand of hot peppery condiment. Added sparingly to cocktail sauce for seafood, to salad dressings and wherever extra "zip" is desired.

Table d'Hote (täbl dōt′)–Fixed price meal. A complete meal as described on the menu for a set price, as distinguished from à la carte listings in which each item is priced separately.

Tablespoon–A large spoon used for eating soup, for service at the table or as a measuring unit in cooking. Abbreviated as tbs. or tbsp.

Tablespoonful (tablespoonsful or tablespoonfuls)–As much as a level tablespoon will hold (not heaping). Four tablespoonsful equal ¼ cup.

Taco (takko)–Mexican specialty popular throughout the Southwest. Like a turnover made with an outer covering of corn meal batter and a filling of highly-seasoned ground meat. Fried in deep fat.

Tallahassee Hush Puppies–Southern. See Hush Puppies.

Tamale (tä mäll′ē̄e)–Popular Mexican dish of cooked cereal (usually corn meal) and ground or chopped meat. Filling may be of chicken, veal or beef seasoned with minced onion, chili powder, garlic, salt, bay leaves and water to mixing consistency, all cooked together. The envelope-shaped covering is made by mixing corn meal, fat, salt and soup stock, beaten until light.

"Redi-cut" cornhusks may be bought. Field-grown cornhusks must have both ends removed and husks immersed in cold water while filling is cooking.

To assemble: Wash and dry the cornhusks. Spread the inside with the corn meal mixture. Add one teaspoon of the chili-and-meat mixture. Roll cornhusk like a cigarette and fold both ends over. Stack in a steamer and cook over a low flame about 45 minutes. Always serve piping hot.

Tansy–Associated with immortality, either because of medicinal qualities or because the small yellow flowers retain their appearance when dried. Strong-smelling herb plant.

Tapioca–Granular starchy substance made from the root of the Cassava plant. Used to thicken soups, puddings, etc.

Tarragon–An herb of the aster family whose fragrant leaves are used for seasoning. Fresh leaves may be cut up and mixed with garden salads. Or, they may be added to vinegar to impart the characteristic flavor to salad dressings. See Fines Herbes.

Tartar Sauce

Tartar Sauce (tär′tẽr)–Yellow sauce served with fried or broiled seafood. Made by blending mayonnaise with onion juice, chopped cucumber pickle and capers. May be mixed ahead and kept in the refrigerator until needed. It should be quite thick when served.

Tartare Steak–Raw hamburger, highly seasoned.

Tart–May refer to a miniature open-top pastry shell filled with mincemeat or any fruit filling. Or it may mean a sharp, sour or acidy taste.

Tarte, F. f. (tärt)–Open- faced fruit pie. Small.

Tartelettes, F. f. pl. (tärt lĕt′)–Small fruit or jam tarts. Desserts. If filled with meat mixture, these may be added to hors d'oeuvres assortments.

Tasse, F. f. sg. (täss)–Cup.

T-Bone Steak–Like a porterhouse, but smaller.

Tea–A social gathering in the afternoon at which tea or coffee is served, as opposed to a cocktail party. Afternoon tea is an established institution in such countries as England. Alternate meaning: a beverage served hot or iced.

Tea, Black–India, Java, Ceylon. Leaves are fermented before they are dried. Steeping produces a dark amber liquid.

Tea, Green–Mostly from Japan. Infusion is light-colored.

Tea, Oolong–Formosa. Semi-fermented.

Tea, Orange-Pekoe–Pekoe refers to the downy appearance of the undersides and ends of leaf buds. Leaves for this tea are picked while very young and tender.

Tenderloin–Hindquarters of beef, inside loin.

Tequila*, M. (te kēē′lä)–White Mexican liquor.

Terrapin–Fresh water turtle. Maryland style: pickled and served with Supreme Sauce. Baltimore style: with Madeira Sauce.

Terrine, F. f. (tĕr′een″)–Forcemeat stuffing molded in an earthenware jar. Served cold, like a paste.

Terrine de Foie Gras, F. f. (tĕr′een″de fwä′grä)–Imported gooseliver paste in jars. Best-known brands come from Strassbourg.

Tete, F. f. (tait)–Head.

Tete de veau, F. f. (tait de vō′)–Calf's head.

Thé, F. (tā)–Tea.

Thermometers–Instruments for measuring temperatures in various places where foods are involved, such as: frozen food freezers, refrigerators, ovens, meat thermometers for roasting and baking, and candy thermometers for use in boiling liquids on top of the range. These take the guesswork out of food preparation.

Thiamine (thī′e meen)–Also known as vitamin B_1. See vitamins.

Thon, F. m. (tŏn)—Tunafish, found in salt water.

Thousand Island Dressing—Colorful salad dressing made by blending mayonnaise, chili sauce, chives, vinegar, pepper, and paprika. Similar to Russian Dressing.

Thuringer Cervelat (thŭr ĭngĕr sĕr vĕ lät)—Medium-dry summer sausage.

Thyme—Fragrant herb of the mint family. Its leaves, fresh, may be combined in a Bouquet Garni or in Fines Herbes. Dried leaves are combined with other herbs for stuffings or as seasonings for soups, stews, etc.

Tidbit—A small taste, as an appetizer or canapé.

Timbales—Sugarless custards baked in timbale molds. Milk may be replaced with meat stock or vegetable purée. Eggs are the thickening agent. Savory seasoning is used. This term is sometimes used to describe forcemeat cooked in straight-sided deep molds, contents turned out of mold before serving. Cooked by oven-poaching and not browned.

Timbale Shells, Timbale Cases or Rosettes—Flour, salt, sugar, egg and irradiated evaporated milk mixed to a smooth, creamy batter. Fluted timbale iron is heated in deep fat to about 370°F., excess fat removed, then iron is dipped in batter, several times if necessary to get a good coating. Dipped again in hot deep fat until done (two or three minutes). These cases may be filled with creamed oysters, chicken or sweetbreads, a creamed vegetable or with fresh or cooked fruit. The latter are topped with whipped cream or powdered sugar.

Tipsy Pudding—Similar to Tipsy Trifle. Slice small cup cakes or sponge cake into a serving dish. Pour over this soft custard and sherry, or sherry-flavored custard. Let stand 15 minutes, then chill.

Toasting—Application of direct heat until surface is browned, as of bread, etc.

Toddy—Drink of liquor, sugar, water and seasoning. Hot or cold.

Tokay, H.—Superlative wine from old Hungary. The sweetest is also the best. Similar to the great sauternes of the area, including the German Aszu.

Tom and Jerry—A long drink of liquor (brandy, rum) sugar, nutmeg, hot water. Fine for Aprés Ski.

Tom Collins—Tall drink of gin or rum, sugar, lemon juice, seltzer. Served over ice in tall glasses.

Tomato—Juicy fruit of a tender annual plant. Usually produces large red fruits. Fresh ripe tomatoes: slices or wedges are added to vegetable salads. Tasty. Colorful. Rich in vitamin C. Canned: whole, sliced or puréed. Widely used in soups, chowders and sauces, especially in Spanish, Italian and Mexican foods. Condiments: Ripe tomatoes are the chief ingredient in catsup and chili sauce. Green tomatoes are chopped for picalilli or blended with other vegetables in chow chow. New tomatoes bred at U-Cal in Davis, Calif. by crossing traditional round tomatoes with Italian plum tomatoes produced a type which can be garnered by mechanical pickers. Easy to slice mechanically for canning. Small red or yellow cherry or plum are pleasing garnishes.

Topping—Decorative and tasty finish served on foods. Examples: meringue on open-faced pies; whipped cream on berries, etc.

Torte, G. (tōr′tä), or **tourte**, F. f. (tōort)—Rich, sweet cake resembling date sticks.

Tortillas, M. (tōr tē′yäz)—Griddle cakes, Mexican style.

Tortue, F. f. (tōr tōō′)—Turtle.

Tournedos, F. m. (tōōr′nē dō)—Round-shaped beef tenderloin.

Tréacle—Like molasses. Dark. British. Made during the process of refining sugar.

Trichina—Very small worms whose larvae infest the intestines of humans and the voluntary muscles. Possible source: insufficiently-cooked pork. Symptoms: fever, nausea, diarrhea, muscle pains, general debilitation.

Trifle—Sponge cake or cup cakes soaked in sherry and served with jam.

Tripe—Lining of beef stomach. Useful in making certain kinds of soup, such as Pepper Pot.

Triple Sec* or Cointreau*, F. (trĭpl sĕk′or kwan′trō)—Sweet orange cordial originally imported from France.

Trout—A large group of fishes related to salmon, but grown chiefly in fresh waters. Rainbow, Brook, Brown and Speckled are the most famous American trout, chiefly found in the Atlantic Coast areas. Pacific Coast trout: Steelhead, Cut-throat and Dolly Varden. For commercial service, sizes weighing about a pound to a pound and a half are preferred. Raised commercially on trout farms, as in Idaho, trout are fed scientifically to produce the best flavor and most rapid growth (for tenderness). Large quantities of specified sizes may be bought as for banquet service, thereby simplifying the problem of portion control.

Truffles, F. f. pl. (troof)—Truffles.

Truffles—Fungus-like mushrooms which grow underground, chiefly in France. Used as a garnish or seasoning. Excellent in meat dishes, but also used in making chocolate candy.

Truite, F. f. (trōō ēēt′)—Trout.

Truss—To skewer or tie wings and legs of poultry before roasting.

Try out—To cook fat until the oil is rendered out, as in lard.

Turbot (tŭr bŏt)—Halibut.

Turkey—Domesticated wild fowl native to America. The Bronze turkey is largest. Young toms (males) may weigh up to 25 lb. Young hens tip the scales at 16 lb. Bourbon Red and White Holland are good varieties. The Beltsville variety, developed by the U. S. Dept. of Agriculture at Beltsville, Md., is smaller (5 to 8 lb.), but has a bigger breast and yields more white meat. Turkey used to be a Thanksgiving and holiday specialty, served here as the British and Continentals employ goose. Its popularity in restaurants is so great that turkey is now a year-around menu staple. Roast turkey, served hot, makes a desirable entrée, with or without stuffing. Sliced cold, it's an entree when combined with vegetable salad. Sandwiches, hot or cold, sell well. Chopped or diced, turkey may be creamed, put in casseroles, hashed, or made into croquettes. Ground turkey, made into gelatin mousse, is fine for buffet dishes.

Turkish Coffee, F. (Cafe Turk)—Strong, sweet black coffee. Thickish. Made with pulverized coffee. Specialty after-dinner beverage.

Turmeric—East Indian plant whose root, ground, is used as a yellow coloring in foods.

Turnovers—Pie crust or puff paste squares filled with meat or fruit, folded diagonally into triangles and baked.

Turtle, Diamond-back—Great delicacy. Source: salt marshes.

Tutti Frutti, I. (tōō'tē frōō″tē)—Mixture of fruits, as in ice cream or cake frosting.

Tuxedo Cocktail—Gin, sweet vermouth and sherry.

Frying pan or skillet should be shallow so that a fried fish may be removed without breaking it up.

119

Udo—California vegetable much like asparagus in shape and growth.

Upside-down cake—Cake pan lined with fruit and syrup (pineapple, apricots, peaches, etc.); batter poured on top. Baked. Cake turned out so that the fruit and syrup are on top. No frosting needed. See also Upside-down Bread, under Breads.

Upside-down cake can be made with a variety of fruits, is often served with a swirl of whipped cream.

Varié, -e, F. (vă rēē ā')—Mixed. A variety, as hors d'oeuvres.

Veal—Meat from young beef cattle less than a year old.

Veal Birds—Thin slices of veal which have been rolled around seasoned stuffing. May be stewed or baked. A strip of bacon may be wrapped around each veal bird and secured with a toothpick.

Veal Schnitzel—Vienna veal cutlets. Seasoned flour pounded into the meat as for Swiss Steak, which see. Pan-fried until brown on both sides. Served with wedges of lemon.

Veau, F. m. (vō)—Veal.

Vegetable Marrow—Like squash.

Vegetarian—A person who subsists entirely on a diet of vegetables and fruits. Some vegetarians eat no animal products at all (milk, butter, eggs) either for reasons of health or because they are opposed to killing animals.

Velouté Sauce, F. (věl ōō tā')—White sauce. Used as a base for many other sauces, as well as for creamed dishes.

Venison—Deer, or reindeer, meat. Game.

Vermicelli, I.—Long, thin, spaghetti-like threads of noodle dough. Used especially in soups.

Vermouth, F. (vĕr mōōth')—Aromatic wine, seasoned with herbs, served as an aperitif or mixed with liquor in many cocktail recipes. Formerly, dry vermouth was made in France; sweet vermouth in Italy. Now both are also made in the United States.

Vermouth Cassis—Cassis, French vermouth and seltzer.

Vermouth Cocktail—Vermouth instead of stronger liquor, orange bitters or Angostura, and perhaps sugar. Iced.

Vert, -e, F. (vair or vairt)—Green.

Vert d'Epinarde, F. (vair dā pēē när)—Green food coloring made of spinach.

Verts haricots, F. (vair tărĭcō)—Green Beans, String Beans.

Viands—Food, victuals. Especially choice dishes.

Vichy*, F. (vēē shēē')—Mineral water from France.

Vichy, à la, F.—Purée: mashed carrots. Vichy salts. Carrots: cut in discs, stewed or cooked in broth, with butter and sugar added.

Vichyssoise, F. (vēē shēē swäs)—Cold potato soup made of puréed potatoes, finely chopped leeks and onion, butter, carrot, chicken stock, milk and cream. Served thoroughly chilled. Garnished with chopped chives.

Victor Hugo Sauce, F.—Egg yolks blended with butter, vinegar, lemon juice, meat stock, horseradish, seasoned with tarragon.

Vienna Bread

Vienna Bread—Glazed crust. Thick cylindrical loaf. White, with or without milk. Slashed across the top.

Vienna Rolls—Crisp rolls similar to French rolls.

Vienna Sausage—Lightly smoked beef sausage, ¾ in. diameter. Ready cooked.

Vinaigrette Sauce, F. (vē nā grait')—Salad dressing made of vinegar, oil and herbs, blended with chopped hard-cooked eggs and chopped pickles. May also be used over hot cooked foods, such as asparagus or spinach.

Vin, F. m. (văn)—Wine.

Vinegar—A sour liquid containing acetic acid, made by fermenting cider, wine, malt, etc. Widely used in cooking and in making salad dressings. A condiment and a preservative.

Vintage—Grapes or wine of the best seasons. Premium.

Virginia Ham—Fine-flavored ham cured and smoked by special recipes. Prized for holidays and banquets.

Virginia Salad—Diced Virginia ham, endive, seasonings, all arranged on a bed of crisp lettuce. German dressing.

Vitamins—Generally considered to be essential constituents which contribute to the human body's well-being and health. The most important vitamins are:

Vitamin A—Carotene, which promotes growth and general vigor, improves appetite and digestion. Adds resistance to infection, especially in respiratory passages, gastro-intestinal tract, and eyes (helps to prevent night blindness and corneal ulcers).
Sources: Whole milk, butter, cheese, egg yolk, cod liver oil, green leafy vegetables, green beans and peas, yellow vegetables (corn, carrots, sweet potatoes).

Vitamin B—Niacin or nicotinic acid. Nourishes nerve and brain tissues. Perishable during long cooking or intense heat. Promotes appetite and digestion. Aids in maintaining vigorous health. Deficiency may result in nervous disorders, diabetes, neuritis, thyroid disorders and, in extreme cases, beri-beri. Sources: Whole grain cereals, peas, beans, buttermilk, cabbage, spinach, egg yolk, honey and yeast.

Vitamin C—Ascorbic Acid; the anti-scurvy vitamin. Promotes good circulation of the blood and oxygen metabolism. Deficiency may cause loss of weight, shortness of breath, physical weakness, as well as tendency to bruise easily and to hemorrhage. Most cases of tooth decay are due to vitamin C deficiency, as are swelling and redness of the gums. Vitamin C is not stored in the body, therefore a new supply must be eaten every day. Sources: Green peppers, oranges, lemons, tomatoes (raw or canned), bananas and raw fruits in general, sprouted grains, green leafy vegetables, potatoes, liver and raw cabbage.

Vitamin D—The sunshine vitamin is also called the "anti-richitic" vitamin. Regulates calcium and mineral metabolism. Lack of it may cause rickets, deformity of bones in children and defective teeth. Deficient amounts cause muscular weakness, instability of the nervous system and lower resistance against disease. Sources: Cod liver oil, haliver oil, egg yolk, whole milk, spinach, irradiated foods, and exposure to sunshine. Overdoses can cause premature symptoms of senility and arterio-sclerosis.

Vitamin E—Fertility vitamin. Necessary to reproduction. Lack of it also tends to cause arthritis, cerebral hemorrhage, dermatitis, eczema and to affect eye motility. Sources: Whole grain cereals, milk, lettuce, watercress and raw fruits.

Vitamin F—Aids circulation and improves skin tone. Promotes growth. Deficiency can result in dry skin, constipation, fragile bones, tiring easily. Sources: Oats, rye, milk and cod liver oil.

Vitamin G—Necessary to normal calcium metabolism. Deficiency may result in underdevelopment, eye cataracts, calcium deposits (as in blood vessel walls and joints), secondary anemia and, in extreme cases, pellagra. Sources: Cereal grain, brewer's yeast, eggs.

Vodka, R.—Clear spirit distilled from grain. Much used in Russia and gaining popularity in the United States. Used to be made in Russia and imported stateside. Now also made in this country by licensed agreements to use Russian formulas. Leaves no after-scent, its drinkers say. Very popular in Martinis and Bloody Marys.

Voiture, en, F. (ŏn vwä′tūre)—Meats carted on a heat retaining wagon and served at the table, as prime ribs.

Volaille, F. f. (vol′eye)—Poultry.

Volnay*, F. (vŏl nä′)—Delicate red Burgundy wine from the Volnay region. Pronounced fragrance. En Chevret, Les Angles, Le Clos de Chenes, Carelle-sous-la-Chapelle and several other names are associated with it.

Volga Cocktail—Vodka, grenadine, orange-and-lemon juices. Iced.

Wafers—Thin, flat, crisp crackers. Served with soup or salads. Used for spreads as appetizers. This term also applies to thin round candies, as mint wafers, chocolate covered mint wafers, etc.

Waffles—Batter-cakes baked in special grid-type iron which has two plates that close to retain heat and bake the waffle between them. Delicate, yet crisp texture. Many kinds may be made by mixing nuts or fruits with the batter. Still greater variety may be obtained by serving a choice of toppings: butter, syrup, honey, preserves, jams. For the luncheon menu, waffles may be used instead of toast for creamed chicken and similar foods. Waffle shortcake can be made by spreading fresh fruit between two layers of waffles; topping with whipped cream and decorating with fresh fruit, such as orange sections or slices, or whole strawberries, etc.

Waldorf Salad—An historic standby. Diced apples, celery, chopped nuts, and a dressing of blended mayonnaise and whipped cream. Served on a bed of crisp lettuce, of course, and garnished with colorful fresh fruit (raspberry, loganberry, strawberry, etc.).

War Mein, C.—Chinese dish of fried noodles, bean sprouts, mushrooms, peanut oil or sesame oil, soy, cornstarch, and soup stock.

Washington Chowder—Soup of white cream sauce, corn, tomatoes, onions and potatoes, seasoned with herbs.

Washington Pie—Cake with raspberry or loganberry jam between layers.

Wassail Bowl—Christmas specialty which may be made in several ways. Basically it is hot wine spiced and dressed up. An excellent recipe calls for claret, heated but not boiled; sugar, ground ginger, nutmeg, allspice, cinnamon, cloves and just enough hot water to blend the spices. The whites and yolks of fourteen eggs are beaten separately, then blended. The mixture is poured into a punch bowl and stirred as the hot spiced wine is added. Makes a very pretty as well as tasty beverage. Looks festive if the bowl is surrounded with a circle of holly greens and berries.

Wedges—He-man sandwiches that are almost a full meal. Sausage, sliced green peppers and onions; all grilled and tucked between two halves of a large hard roll. Featured especially by quick foodservice places catering to "the boys" or to an active outdoor crowd, as near a marina or other spot that attracts athletes. Also called "Hero Sandwiches," "Hoagy Sandwiches," and "Submarines." Italian Wedges are made with cold ingredients: salami, provolone cheese, shredded lettuce, etc., on Italian wedge rolls or bread.

Welsh Rarebit—Fondue of cheese cooked until smooth, combined with beaten eggs, condiments such as Worcestershire Sauce, butter and sometimes beer.

Western Sandwich—Chopped ham, green pepper, onions, mixed with beaten eggs and fried like scrambled eggs but allowed to brown on both sides without stirring.

Whip, whips—Delicate desserts made of sieved and sweetened fruit pulp blended with stiffly beaten egg whites and sugar. Whipped cream may be added. Examples: Prune Whip, Peach Whip, Apricot Whip.

Whipping—Beating rapidly to increase volume by mixing in air; as in whipping cream or egg whites.

Whiskey Sour—Cocktail of whiskey, sugar or simple syrup, lemon juice and sliced fruit.

Whitefish—White or silvery freshwater fish found in the lakes of northeastern United States. Good fried or baked. Also available smoked; a tasty addition to cold plates.

White Lady Cocktail—Gin, Cointreau, lemon juice.

White Mountain Cake—Light delicate-textured cake made with whites of eggs only (not yolks). Baked in layers. May be put together with any kind of filling and frosted to suit. Wonderful stand-by. Nearly foolproof even for beginners.

White Sauce—Cooking fat, flour and seasonings with milk. Served over boiled vegetables or used as a base for many other sauces.

Whitings—European sea fish of the cod family.

Weiner Schnitzel—See Vienna Schnitzel.

Wild Rice—See Rice.

The chef's whip is a basic tool that comes in several sizes; the one selected will depend on the size of the mixture.

Wines

Wines—Fermented juice of grapes. Many kinds: Aperitifs, Bordeaux, Burgundies, Champagnes, Chiantis, fortified wines, Madeiras, Moselles, Muscatines, Ports, Sauternes, and Sherries. May also be classified as "still" or "sparkling" wines; or "dry," "semi-sweet" or "sweet." Specialties include Japanese plum wine, "sake" or "saki" (rice wine), etc.

Imported wines come chiefly from France, Germany, Spain, Italy, Portugal and Greece.

American wines, which many say are superior to all but the best imports, are made from grapes grown on imported vinefera vines, labrusca native vines, or improved grafted varieties.

California has made tremendous strides in wine production. Many thousands of vineyard acres are irrigated (actually "misted" to prevent grapes and vines from drying out during hot weather). Mild winters prevent damage to vines. Most important types of wine are being made in that state.

New York State's wine growing area specializes in grapes grown on vines improved from the native labrusca, which is immune to the dreaded filoxera (mildew) infestations that threaten the vinefera vineyards. Chief types of "wanted" wines are also produced here.

Several other states produce some wines, but none compete with New York and California for quantity.

Worcestershire Sauce*—Trademarked condiment served with meats at the table or added to stews and casserole foods before cooking.

Wormwood—See Absinthe.

126

Yam Puff—Casserole-cooked yams. Southern.

Yams—Much like sweet potatoes, but juicier. Tropical climbing plant.

Yankee Pot Roast—Braised beef served with cooked vegetables (onions, potatoes, carrots, celery, etc.). May be served with corn fritters, if desired.

Yearlings—Beef cattle just over a year old. Tender meat.

Yeast, compressed—Used for "quick-rising" bread, rolls, pastries. In fresh compressed yeast, the yeast plants are alive and ready for action. Must be refrigerated until used. Stale compressed yeast is streaky, slippery and has an unpleasant odor. Never use it.

Yeast, dry—Mass of yeast plants mixed with corn meal and/or flour and dried to make them inactive. As yeast plants will live for considerable time, yet cannot grow without moisture, dry yeast cakes will keep for many weeks. When warmth, moisture, food and air are supplied, the yeast plants require time to become active. Dry yeast, therefore, is used for doughs which stand overnight to rise. The action of yeast is to form alcohol and carbon dioxide during the process of fermentation. The bubbles of carbon dioxide cause the dough to rise and become light in texture, prior to baking. During baking, oven heat causes the air bubbles to expand, thereby making the dough even lighter.

Yellow Sauce—Variation obtained by adding uncooked beaten egg yolks to white sauce.

Yorkshire Bock or Buck—Welsh rabbit with poached eggs and broiled bacon. Served with anchovy toast.

Yorkshire Eggs—Casserole dish of sliced hard-cooked eggs covered with light, fluffy batter and baked like a soufflé.

Yorkshire Pudding—Served with roast beef. British specialty. Pudding is made of flour, salt and milk blended with well-beaten eggs for leavening. Baked in shallow pan coated with roast drippings, then cut into squares and laid around the roast to absorb gravy flavor. May also be bought ready-made, in cans.

Youngberry—Cross between dewberry and loganberry.

Zabaglione (zä bä yō′nee)—Also called Sabaillone. This may be either a dessert served chilled in sherbet cups, or made thinner for use as a dessert sauce. Made by beating egg yolks and honey until thick and lemon-colored in the top of a double boiler. Marsala wine or sweet sherry (2 tablespoons to a batch requiring 4 egg yolks) is added gradually as the mixture heats. Must be beaten continuously to prevent "breaking." The above mixture makes the sauce. For the dessert, add beaten whites of egg at the last, to produce a fluffy mixture.

Zeltinger*, G. (zĕl′tĭngĕr)—Dry fruity Moselle wine.

Zinfandel (zĭn fän dĕl′)—Wine made in California from Zinfandel grapes which are unknown in Europe. Similar to Beaujolais. Agreeable, light-colored, slightly spicy wine. An excellent table wine, especially good with luncheon dishes.

Ziti—Italian dish of macaroni boiled, blended with tomato sauce, Mozzarella cheese and Romano, then baked at 425°F.

Zombie—A knocker-outer drink containing 4½ oz. of assorted rums, pineapple and lime juices, apricot liqueur, falernum syrup (black raspberry flavor), and garnished with orange slices and mint. Served in a 14-oz. glass with straws. One to a customer. Who could "carry" more?

Zucchini, I. (tsoo kee′nee)—Long slender green Italian squash. Delicate texture. Avoid overcooking. May be boiled and served with butter sauce, or fried in butter. Delightful with veal or chicken.

Zwieback, G. (tswee′bäk)—Hard, crisp German biscuits. Twice toasted. Similar to rusks.

Zymosis—Fermentation. Avoid unwanted fermentation by proper care of food. See Botulus Bacillus.

FOREIGN WORDS AND PHRASES

à la, au, aux—Prepared or served in a certain style.

à l'Ancienne—Old style.

à la Bourgeoise—Family style.

à la mode—Literally, "in the fashion." "Pie a la mode" is pie served with ice cream. "Beef a la mode" comes with a scoop of mashed potatoes.

Artichaut—Artichoke.

Asperge—Asparagus.

Au gratin—Baked with a topping of crumbs and/or grated cheese.

Bisque—Thickened soup, usually made from shellfish. Or ice cream containing finely chopped nuts.

Blanquette—White meat in cream sauce that has been thickened with eggs.

Bombe Glaçée—Molded dessert of vari-colored ice creams or ices.

Bouchées—Small pastry shells filled with creamed meat or fish. Literally, "a mouthful."

Café au lait—Coffee with milk.

Café noir—Black coffee.

Canard—Duck.

Canapé—Appetizer. Usually a highly-seasoned spread on crackers, bread or toast cut in fancy shapes.

Caviar—Black or red roe from sturgeon, salmon or other fish.

Champignons—Mushrooms.

Chaud-froid—Jellied sauce. Literally, "hot-cold."

Compote Stewed fruits in syrup.

Coq au vin Chicken cooked with wine. The French are famous for it.

Croûtons—Small cubes of toasted or butter-fried bread served with soup.

De, or d'—Of.

Demitasse—Half a cup. Small cup of black coffee usually served at the close of dinner.

Éclair—Pastry shell filled with whipped cream or custard.

En brochette—On a skewer.

Entrées—Formerly meant small amounts of food served between the heavy courses at a formal dinner. Now usually means the main course of lunch or dinner.

Farci—Stuffed.

Fillets—Long, thin slices or pieces of boneless meat or fish.

Fines Herbes—Minced herbs, assorted: parsley, chives, basil, chervil, and others.

129

Fondant—Basis of French candy, made by boiling sugar to the soft-ball stage, then kneading it to a smooth creaminess. Also used to stuff figs, dates, prunes, etc.

Frappé—Iced or semi-frozen dessert.

Fromage—Cheese.

Gelée—Jelly, or jellied.

Glacé—Frozen or glazed.

Haricots verts—Young green beans.

Hors d'Oeuvres—Canapes or appetizers.

Jambon—Ham.

Jardiniere—Mixed vegetables served in their own sauce.

Julienne—Vegetables cut in thin, matchlike strips, used in clear vegetable soup, salads, stews, casseroles.

Laitue—Lettuce.

Macédoine—Mixture. Usually vegetables or fruits.

Marrons—Chestnuts.

Meringue—Whites of eggs whipped to a standing froth with sugar.

Mousse—Smooth, mossy texture. Applies to finely-ground chicken, ham, etc., molded in gelatin; served in fancy buffets.

Noir—Black. Café noir. Beurre (butter) noir.

Pain—Bread.

Paté—French pastry, patty.

Patisserie—Pastry. Pastry shop.

Pêche—Peach.

Petits Pois—Small green peas.

Piece de Résistance—Main dish of a meal.

Pommes—Apples.

Pommes de terre—Potatoes. Literally, "apples of the earth."

Paté de Foie Gras—Goose liver paste or spread.

Potage—Soup.

Poulet—Chicken.

Purée—Ingredients rubbed through a sieve to a pulp-like consistency, as when making a thick soup. Any thick paste, as tomatoes or mashed potatoes.

Ragout—Thick, highly-seasoned stew.

Réchauffé—Reheated. Warmed over.

Ris de Veau—Sweetbreads.

Rissoles—Minced fish or meat rolled in thin pastry and fried.

Rôti—Roast.

Rôti à la poele—Cooked in a casserole.

Salade—Salad.

Sorbet—Frozen punch. Water ice.

Soufflé—Means "puffed up." Delicate baked custard which may contain cheese, minced meat, fish or fruit.

130

Tarte—Pastry tart or shell, usually filled with stewed fruit or jam.

Tartelette—Small tart.

Timbale—Unsweetened custard seasoned with fish, poultry or meat. Baked in a mold.

Timbale Case—Fried batter shells in which creamed mixtures or desserts are served.

Tourte—Tart or pie.

Truffles—Species of mushroom-like fungi which grow in clusters below the ground. Seasoning. Garnish.

Tutti-Frutti—Mixed fruits. Usually chopped.

Velouté—Velvety smooth; usually a sauce which may be served with meats or vegetables. Also used as a base for other sauces.

DEFINITIONS OF CULINARY TERMS

Bake: to cook with indirect heat in an oven.

Baste: to pour liquid or drippings over meat while cooking.

Beat: to whip. To make fluffy by adding air. Examples: to beat egg whites until stiff with a wire whisk, eggbeater or electric mixer. Also to make smooth by whipping with a spoon or fork.

Boil: to cook in a liquid which bubbles during time called for by recipe, at 212°F.

Braise: to brown meat or vegetables in a small amount of fat and cook covered in an oven or on top of the range, adding liquid as needed to prevent scorching or burning.

Broil: to cook over or under direct heat.

Blanch: to dip in boiling hot water, but not to cook.

Caramelize: to cook granulated sugar until it is melted and turns brownish. Cook slowly over low heat to prevent burning.

Chop: to cut in small pieces with a knife, cleaver or chopper.

Cream: to soften shortening as the first step in baking a cake. To blend ingredients together.

Crisp: to immerse vegetables (celery, lettuce) in cold water. Or to heat crackers and cereals in the oven until crisp.

Cube: to cut in small squares.

Cut in shortening: to blend cold shortening by cutting it into flour with two silver or stainless steel table knives. Produces flaky pastry as opposed to the crumbly type obtained when shortening and flour are blended by hand.

Dot: to scatter bits (of butter or cheese) over food to be cooked.

Dredge: to cover food with a dusting of flour or crumbs.

Fillet: to remove bone from meat or fish.

Fold in: to add whipped cream, stiffly-beaten egg whites, etc. into mixture with a folding motion to preserve the air bubbles. Examples: soufflés, chiffon pies, fluffy desserts like zabaglione.

Fry: to cook in hot fat on top of the range.

Frying in deep fat: to cook in a large amount of hot fat, as French fried potatoes, fritters, etc.

Frying, pan frying: to cook in a small amount of fat.

Garnish: to decorate food. Examples: sprigs of watercress or parsley on salads; maraschino cherries, fresh fruit or nuts on desserts.

Grate: to rub on a grater. Examples: lemon or orange rind for cake or biscuits; nutmeg for seasoning; carrots for gelatinized salads; horseradish, for condiments.

Julienne: to cut in narrow strips.

Knead: to fold dough firmly with the palms of the hands, turning it over each time. Improves texture, as in making bread.

Marinate: to coat or cover with a dressing, such as oil-vinegar or French dressing for a period of time in advance of serving. Purpose: to allow food to absorb the flavor.

Mince: to cut or chop very fine, but not in a grinder.

Parboil: to boil in water until partly cooked.

Pare: to remove skin of fruit or vegetables with a knife.

Peel: to remove skin, as by a mechanical potato peeler.

Poach: to cook in liquid just below boiling.

Purée: to rub food through a coarse sieve; to separate pulp from outer covering, as peas, tomatoes, fruit.

Roast: to cook in an oven with indirect dry heat.

Scald: to heat liquid until hot but not boiling. Usually milk.

Score: to make shallow slits in the surface of meat or fish, lengthwise, diagonally or criss-cross. Example: ham prepared for baking.

Shred: to cut in thin pieces, as in preparing cabbage for coleslaw.

Skewer: to fasten meat or vegetables together in preparation for broiling. Also used to close a chicken after stuffing it prior to roasting. Term also applies to the spike used, wood or metal.

Steam: to cook over steam or in a steam-jacketed kettle.

Steep: to let stand in hot liquid (as tea) in order to extract flavor and color.

Stir: to blend ingredients with a circular motion. Also to keep food in motion to prevent it from scorching or sticking to the pan while cooking. Especially important when cooking any sauce or gravy thickened with flour, cornstarch or eggs.

Toast: to brown by direct heat in an electric toaster, a broiler or a hot oven. Examples: cold waffles or stale pound cake are freshened and made tasty by toasting. Almonds are usually toasted to make them crisp.

Whip: to beat rapidly, as eggs, cream, thickened sauces or gravies. Also a class of desserts called "whips."

EQUIVALENT WEIGHTS AND MEASURES

3 teaspoons	equal	1 tablespoon
4 tablespoons	equal	¼ cup
16 tablespoons	equal	1 cup
½ cup	equals	1 gill
4 gills	equal	1 pint
2 pints	equal	1 quart
4 cups	equal	1 quart
4 quarts	equal	1 gallon
8 quarts	equal	1 peck
4 pecks	equal	1 bushel
16 ounces	equal	1 pound

To measure liquids, use glass or plastic cups which are marked both in ounces and in cups. Available in half-pint, pint, and quart sizes.

Allspice, ground	1 ounce =	4 tablespoons
Almonds, shelled	1 pound =	2½ cups
Apricots, dried	1 pound =	3 cups; 6 cups when cooked
Bacon, medium strip	1 pound =	about 30 full thin slices
Bacon, wide strip	1 pound =	15 full thin slices
Baking powder	1 ounce =	3 tablespoons
Beef, raw	1 pound, lean makes 3 or 4 servings	
Bread, 1¼ lb. loaf	=	15 slices ½-in. thick $\pm$
2 lb. loaf	=	24 slices ½-in. thick $\pm$
Long sandwich loaf	=	36-40 slices ¼-in. thick
Butter	1 pound =	about two cups
	¼-lb. stick =	about ½ cup
Chocolate	1 pound =	16 squares
	1 square =	5 tablespoons when grated
Coffee	1 pound =	5 cups of ground coffee
Egg whites	1 cup =	8-11 whites, depending on size
Egg yolks	1 cup =	12 yolks, depending on size
Eggs, whole	1 cup =	4 to 6 eggs, according to size
	1 pound =	8 to 9 eggs (without shells)
Lard	1 pound =	2 cups
Lemons	1 pound =	3 to 5 lemons, depending on size
Oatmeal	1 pound =	3 cups, dry measure
Oils	1 pound =	2 cups
Olives	1 quart =	60 to 70 depending on size
Peanut Butter	1 pound =	1¾ cups $\pm$
Peanuts, shelled	1 pound =	2¾ cups $\pm$
Pecans, shelled	1 pound =	3 to 4 cups $\pm$

Rice	1 pound =	2 cups
Sugar (brown)	1 pound =	2½ cups unless very moist
(granulated)	1 pound =	2 cups
(powdered)	1 pound =	2½ cups $\pm$
(cubes)	1 pound =	50-70, depending on size
Tea	1 pound =	6½ cups of dry tea

CALORIC VALUES OF ALCOHOLIC & SOFT DRINKS

Kind of beverages	Calories
Benedictine and similar cordials	75 per ounce
Brandies	75 per ounce
Rum, Gin, Scotch	75 per ounce
Bourbon, Rye Whiskey	85 per ounce
Champagnes	30 per ounce
Wines (Bordeaux, Chablis, etc.)	25 per ounce
Port	50 per ounce
Sherry	45 per ounce
Ale	150 per 8 ounces
Beer	100 per 8 ounces
Sweet Cider	100 per 8 ounces
Gingerale	150 per 8 ounces
Coca-Cola	60 per bottle
Root Beer	75 per bottle
Sparkling water, club soda, etc.	0 no food value

NEW WORDS

NEW WORDS

NEW WORDS

NEW WORDS

NEW WORDS

NEW WORDS